Brownie Fun!

Over 140 Exciting Mini-Treat Ideas
And Delicious Recipes!

Dear Friend,

There is nothing like the aroma of homemade brownies to bring people to the kitchen. When it comes to an easy treat you can bake and enjoy at a moment's notice, brownies can't be beat. But brownies are more than just convenient and delicious. In *Brownie Fun!*, there are brownies and mini treats that look just as great as they taste. With over 140 easy-to-make designs and delicious recipes inside, you'll discover that brownies and mini treats are the ideal decorated desserts for any celebration.

Just look at the cover to see a sample of the many surprises inside. No plain square brownies here—instead, you'll see terrific shapes like sailboats, teddy bears and even a "brownie sundae", bursting with color and perfect for any party.

No one loves brownies more than kids, and in *Brownie Fun!* you'll find dozens of ideas for theme birthday parties that will wow them. Create a bug celebration featuring bees, butterflies and a basket filled with brownie "dirt" and gummy worms. Greet the birthday princess with a royal carriage and crowns studded with candy jewels. Or delight everyone with brownies on a stick, made in our new Brownie Pops mold. These round brownies are great for dipping in candy and colorful toppings. Look for them throughout the book as space aliens, volcanos, penguins and more.

The great colors in *Brownie Fun!* are as surprising as the shapes. You'll be amazed at how simple touches like a squeeze of Drizzle Icing or a sprinkling of Dusting Sugar can make your brownies stand out. If you think a brownie can't be as dazzling as any other treat, check out our section of holiday designs. The color really pops from pastel Easter eggs to Halloween cauldrons in neon green.

The biggest surprise of all may be seeing brownies turn up at big events like weddings and showers. In The Beauty of Brownies section, you'll see how easy it is to dress up brownies with elegant candy bows and monograms, beautiful icing flowers and stenciled sugar designs that will delight your guests.

Brownie Fun! also brings you flavors as exciting as the designs. This is the perfect place to find sensational new recipes that will make any celebration special. From classic fudge brownies to delicious new tastes like caramel macadamia nut, chocolate mint and even chipotle, you'll find something delicious to thrill everyone.

It's time to create your best brownies ever. Turn to *Brownie Fun!* often for party treats that will delight your friends and family.

Marvin Oakes
President
Wilton Enterprises

Credits

Creative Director
Daniel Masini

Art Director/Cake Designer
Steve Rocco

Decorating Room Supervisor
Cheryl Brown

Senior Cake Decorators
Mary Gavenda
Susan Matusiak

Cake Decorators
Jenny Jurewicz ◆ Diane Knowlton
Mark Malak ◆ Tracey Wurzinger
Michele Poto ◆ Kathy Krupa

Recipe Development
Nancy Siler
Gretchen Homan
Michaela Gragert

Editor/Writer
Jeff Shankman

Writers
Mary Enochs
Marita Seiler

Production Manager
Challis Yeager

Graphic Design/Production
Courtney Kieras

Photography
Dale DeBolt Photography
Black Box Studios

Food Stylist
Susie Skoog

Photo Stylist
Carey Thornton

Creative Services Assistant
Judi Graf

Product Development/Publications
Tina Celeste

IN U.S.A.
Wilton Industries, Inc.
2240 West 75th Street
Woodridge, IL 60517
www.wilton.com
Retail Customer Orders:
Phone: 800-794-5866 ◆ Fax: 888-824-9520
Online: www.wilton.com
Class Locations:
Phone: 800-942-8881
Online: www.wilton.com/classes

IN CANADA
Wilton Industries, Canada, Ltd.
98 Carrier Drive
Etobicoke, Ontario M9W5R1 Canada
Retail Customer Orders:
Phone: 416-679-0798
Class Locations:
Phone: 416-679-0790, ext. 200
E-mail: classprograms@wilton.ca

¡SE HABLA ESPAÑOL!
Para mas informacion, marque 800-436-5778

p. 45

Table of Contents

p. 70

p. 93

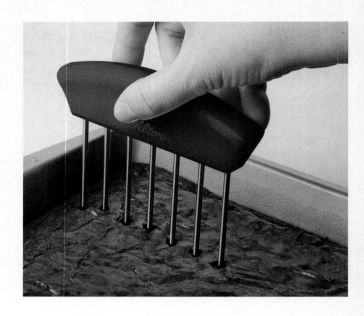

Begin Your Brownies!

As you'll see throughout *Brownie Fun!*, brownies can do so much more than just taste great. For brownies that will make your party feel like a special occasion or look fancy enough to give, you need to prepare them properly, cut them with care and dress them up just right.

In this section, we'll help you create brownies with a perfect texture and an even shape that will look great on the plate. Also, you will discover easy techniques for dressing up a brownie. See how to add color and flavor with quick drizzling and stenciling ideas. Add fun touches like flowers and faces. And create the ideal brownie gift with our exciting presentation ideas. You'll be surprised how a few quick tricks can make such a difference in the brownies you serve!

Brownie Basics

Brownies are very user-friendly. They mix easily and bake up dependably delicious. But for brownies that must look as good as they taste, it pays to follow some easy steps for baking.

Preparing the Batter

Brownies are one of the easiest baked treats to mix. All the batter preparation is done by hand, so all the equipment you need is a large mixing bowl and the Batter Blender (p. 104) or a spoon which allows for efficient blending of the ingredients. In just a few minutes, it's easy to produce brownie batter that's ready to go in the oven. Precise measuring of ingredients can make the difference between brownies with a dry or gritty texture and perfectly moist and chewy brownies.

For dry ingredients, spoon into measuring cups, overfilling the top. Level by running a spatula along the top.

For wet ingredients, use glass or plastic see-through measuring cups and spoons. Pour to the exact level needed.

Follow recipe directions for mixing ingredients. Make sure you run your spoon along the entire bowl surface toward the center, to completely blend all ingredients.

Fudgy vs. Cake-like?

The subject of texture can stir up passion among brownie fans. Some love a dense, fudgy brownie with a gooey consistency. Others prefer a fluffier, cake-like texture. Whichever suits your taste—and many of us love them both—keep in mind that for some designs in this book, a higher-volume cake brownie may make it easier to achieve the look you want.

Fudgy Brownies (p. 78)
These ultra-moist brownies are made with 6 times the chocolate of our cake brownie recipe. They bake about ⅔ as high as cake brownies.

Cake Brownies (p. 78)
Fluffy Cake Brownies use cake flour, made of softer wheat, to bake brownies with a more tender, crumb-like texture. Butter and sugar are creamed to bake up fluffier. Cake Brownies are also leavened with baking powder for a softer, lighter consistency.

Preparing the Pan

Your brownies will turn out perfectly when you measure and mix ingredients precisely and prepare the pan following the steps here.

Metal Pans

Prepare pan following recipe directions. Generously grease the inside using a pastry brush or paper towel and solid vegetable shortening. For best results, do not use butter, margarine or liquid vegetable oil. Spread the shortening so that all indentations are covered. Or use Bake Easy Non-Stick Spray or Cake Release to coat the pan—no grease or flour needed.

Pour batter into pan, filling about ½ to ⅔ full. Place pan in pre-heated oven. If you are baking in a pan with a dark surface, you should lower the recommended recipe temperature by 25°F to avoid overbaked and dry brownies.

9 x 9 x 2 in. Covered Brownie Pan   **Teddy Bear Pan**   **9 x 13 in. Sheet Pan**

Silicone Molds

We suggest preparing the mold with non-stick vegetable pan spray before baking. Always place silicone molds on a cookie sheet or jelly roll pan for level baking and easy removal from oven. Pour batter into mold, filling about ½ to ⅔ full. Place mold in pre-heated oven. You may need to add more baking time for some shapes. To remove brownies, allow to cool completely, invert mold and apply gentle pressure to the bottom while gently peeling mold away.

Blossom Brownie Pops Mold   **Silicone Baking Cups**   **Round Brownie Pops Mold**

Choose the Right Pan

Brownies bake best in aluminum pans or silicone molds. In general, metal pans bake brownies with a crunchier edge, silicone bakes with a soft, chewy edge. Whatever your brownie preference, you can count on great baking performance. Both non-stick aluminum and flexible silicone release treats with ease. Wilton has a great selection of brownie bakeware—from traditional square and rectangle pans to fun flowers, hearts, round brownie pops and more. See all the great shapes on p. 104-105.

Baking

It's fun to let kids help when you're making brownies. Every mixing step is done by hand, so brownies are a great first baking experience. But after the batter is poured in the pan, it's important for bakers of any age to pay attention when brownies are in the oven. Be sure to follow your recipe directions closely for oven time and temperature. Remember, oven temperatures may vary—so watch your oven thermometer to prevent overbaked or underbaked brownies.

To test whether brownies are done, insert a toothpick in the center. If the toothpick comes out with a few crumbs attached, brownies are ready. If the toothpick comes out fully coated with batter, brownies need more time. Be sure to retest in 2-3 minutes. Or, for fudgy brownies, the batch is ready when there is a slight gap between the brownies and the sides of the pan. Even if the center looks gooey, the brownies will firm while cooling. Let brownies cool in the pan on a cooling grid.

Cutting

Brownies taste even better when they are presented at their best. A great look starts with a clean cut, free from crumbs and messy edges.

One easy way to cut square or rectangular brownies cleanly is to use the **Perfect Cut Brownie Cutter** (p. 104). Its stainless steel tines perforate the brownie, allowing for a neater cut.

NOTE: For recipes in this book, serving amounts are based on 2 or 3 in. square portions

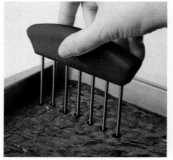

1. Insert the tines into the pan of warm brownies, scoring where you want each cut.

2. Let cool completely, then cut along the score lines.

3. Remove brownies from pan using an angled spatula or brownie lifter.

Cookie cutters are excellent for cutting brownies in a variety of shapes. You can cut brownies using high-sided cutters like our Comfort Grip shapes or our deep handled Combo Cutters. You can also use shorter cutters like our plastic designs to guide you as you complete the cut with a knife. Whatever type of cutter you use, cutters should first be sprayed with a non-stick cooking spray.

Using High-Sided Cutters
Touch cutter to brownie surface. Push straight down, then remove cutter. Run a knife along cut area, then remove brownie with angled spatula or brownie lifter.

Using Shorter Cutters
Touch cutter to brownie surface. Run a knife along cutter shape, then remove brownie with angled spatula or brownie lifter.

To cut and release brownies with one tool, try our spring-action **Push 'N Pop Cutter** (p. 106).

1. Push down to cut brownie.

2. Lift away, then press down on the plunger to pop out your perfectly-shaped brownie.

3. Your brownie is ready to decorate and serve. Use the Push 'N Pop Cutter for cookies and cereal treats, too.

Storage

With their higher moisture content, brownies can easily become dry and crumbly if not stored properly. Covering the brownies is a must! After you've cut brownies, you can wrap the pan in aluminum foil or transfer the brownies to an airtight plastic or metal container. Remember that brownies which contain cream cheese or other perishable ingredients must be stored in the refrigerator. Generally, room temperature brownies last for about 3 days, refrigerated brownies about 5 days.

If you are using a larger sealed container, you can stack a large number of brownies. If you are storing brownies at room temperature or presenting as a gift, place Brownie Tissue Squares (p. 111) between each layer. If you are freezing the container, use Non-Stick Parchment Paper (p. 110) When serving, lift out the sheet and transfer to your plate. If you're bringing a batch along to a party, the 9 x 9 x 2 in. Covered Brownie Pan (p. 105) or Ultimate 3-in-1 Caddy (p. 111) are easy ways to protect brownies and a great-looking way to present them to your hostess.

Brownie Tissue Squares

9 x 9 x 2 in Covered Brownie Pan

Ultimate 3-in-1 Caddy

Presentation

Brownie Fun! is all about dressing up brownies for any occasion. Even undecorated brownies make a great impression when you package them in a pretty gift container. Colorful brownie boxes, bags and decorative envelopes are perfect for quick, easy gifting. Just place brownies inside, then add stickers, ribbons and other accents. See p. 111 for exciting presentation products for brownies and mini treats.

Brownie Boxes

Treat Bags

Brownie Envelopes

Brownie Decorating Techniques

Why serve plain brownies when it's so easy to add color, flavor and fun? Here are some simple steps that will take your brownies beyond the ordinary!

Dipping Treats

Serving brownies or mini cakes dipped in Candy Melts and fun toppings tells everyone it's a special occasion. Whether you dip part of the treat or the entire serving, it's a great way to add flavor and color to plain desserts. The Silicone Round Brownie Pops Mold (p. 104) makes treats on a stick that are easy to dip.

Complete Dipping

Partial Dipping with Sprinkles

1. Melt Candy Melts in microwave-safe bowl following package directions, or use the Chocolate Pro Electric Melting Pot. Dip brownie or mini cake in candy.

2. If desired, immediately dip in Brownie Crunch, Sprinkles, non-pareils, chopped nuts, shredded coconut or other toppings.

3. Place treats on cookie sheet covered with parchment paper. Refrigerate until firm. If desired, drizzle completely dipped treats with melted candy in a cut decorating bag; refrigerate until firm.

Combing in Texture

Use the Decorating Triangle to add contoured texture to iced brownies and treats.

1. Cover treats with a slightly thicker coating of icing so the triangle's ridges will not touch the treat.

2. Choose the type of effect you want—wide or narrow, then run that edge of the triangle along the icing to form ridges using a smooth even or wavy motion. Comb immediately after icing, while the icing is soft.

3. Your finished treat will have an exciting textured look.

Marbleizing with Drizzle Icing

Add an exciting design to your iced brownies using colorful Drizzle Icing or Cookie Icing (p. 109) and a toothpick. It's easy to create stylized hearts, feathered lines, starbursts and more.

Feathered Lines

Stylized Hearts

1. Ice brownie smooth with Wilton Brownie Fudge Icing or buttercream icing. Using Wilton Drizzle Icing or Cookie Icing, pipe dots or outlines on top of iced brownie.

2. Drag a toothpick through dots to create elongated heart shapes or through outlines for a feathered line effect.

3. It's easy to create other exciting marbleized designs by piping zigzags and circles in Drizzle Icing or Cookie Icing, then dragging through with a toothpick.

Decorating with Stencils

Stencils are an easy way to make homemade brownies look great for the party or for giving. With the Brownie Stencil Set (p. 110) you can decorate up to a 9 x 13 in. pan, or use side stencils to decorate a single brownie. Add colorful designs with Dusting Sugar (p. 108).

1. Ice brownie and let icing crust slightly. Before starting, refer to directions on stencil package and spray stencil with non-stick cooking spray.

2. Position stencil on brownie. Using a fine mesh strainer or Sugar Shaker, sprinkle Dusting Sugar carefully over stencil openings until filled in.

3. Carefully remove stencil, placing spatula under one side and lifting off.

Covering with Poured Candy and Icings

Give brownies and mini cakes a great-looking finish by pouring or piping toppings over treats on a cooling rack. The candy or icing will dry with a perfectly smooth surface. For a glossier look, try a Ganache Recipe (p. 103), made with Candy Melts and whipping cream.

1. Place cooled brownie or mini cake on cooling grid positioned over cookie sheet or pan. If you're covering a cupcake, turn it bottom side up. For Candy Melts, melt following package directions. If using Brownie Fudge Icing, follow directions on package to reach pouring consistency. For Ready-To-Use Decorator Icing, heat in microwave at Defrost setting (30% power) for 20-30 seconds; stir. Repeat until icing reaches pouring consistency.

2. Pour icing or candy on center of treat using pan or measuring cup. Or, pipe candy or icing from a cut decorating bag; if using ganache, let cool slightly before piping. Cover the treat completely or use your coating as a glaze to simply cover tops and drip over the sides.

3. For candy-covered treats, refrigerate until firm. For icings, let set at room temperature until firm.

Decorating with a Bag & Tip

Preparing the Bag

Decorating bags hold the icing and decorating tip so you can create a variety of decorations. You can choose reusable Featherweight bags, disposable plastic bags or make your own bags from parchment triangles. Use with a coupler to switch to a different tip on the same bag. For complete instructions on working with decorating bags, see www.wilton.com.

Icing Consistency

If the consistency of your icing is not right, your decorations will not be right either. Just a few drops of liquid can make a great deal of difference in your decorating results.

Stiff icing is used for figure piping and stringwork and for decorations like roses, carnations and sweet peas with upright petals. If icing is not stiff enough, flower petals will droop. If icing cracks when piped out, icing is probably too stiff.

Medium icing is used for decorations such as stars, shell borders and flowers with flat petals. If the icing is too stiff or too thin, you will not get the uniformity that characterizes these decorations.

Thin icing is used for decorations such as printing and writing, vines and leaves. Leaves will be pointier, vines will not break and writing will flow easily if you add 1-2 teaspoons light corn syrup to each cup of icing. Thin icing is used to ice treats smooth. Begin with your prepared icing recipe, then add small amounts of the same liquid used in the recipe (usually milk or water) until the proper spreading consistency is reached.

NOTE: Many factors can affect icing consistency, such as humidity, temperature, ingredients and equipment. You may try using different icing consistencies when decorating to determine what works best for you. As a general guideline, if you are having trouble creating the decorations you want and you feel your icing is too thin, add a little more confectioners' sugar; if you feel your icing is too thick, add a little more liquid. In royal icing recipes, if adding more than ½ cup confectioners' sugar to thicken icing, also add 1-2 additional teaspoons of Meringue Powder (p. 110).

Correct Bag Position

The way your decorations curl, point and lie depends not only on icing consistency but also on the way you hold the bag and the way you move it. Bag positions are described in terms of both angle and direction.

Angle

Angle refers to the position of the bag relative to the work surface. There are two basic angle positions, 90° (straight up) and 45° (halfway between vertical and horizontal).

90° angle or straight up, perpendicular to the surface.

45° angle or halfway between vertical and horizontal.

Direction

The angle in relation to the work surface is only half the story on bag position. The other half is the direction in which the back of the bag is pointed. Correct bag direction is easiest to learn when you think of the back of the bag as the hour hand of a clock.

When you hold the bag at a 45° angle to the surface, you can sweep out a circle with the back end of the bag by rolling your wrist and holding the end of the tip in the same spot. Pretend the circle you formed in the air is a clock face. The hours on the clock face correspond to the direction you point the back end of the bag.

Back of bag at 3:00 **Back of bag at 6:00**

The technique instructions that follow will list the correct direction for holding the bag. When the bag direction differs for left-handed decorators, that direction will be listed in parentheses.

One more thing…since most decorating tip openings are the same shape all the way around, there's no right side and wrong side up when you're squeezing icing out of them. However, some tips have irregularly shaped openings. For those you must watch your tip position as well as your bag position.

Tip Techniques

■ ■

With a decorating bag and tip to create piped icing shapes, there's no limit to the exciting brownie designs you can create! It's easy to add fun details for brownie animals, accent plain brownies with beads and shells or create drop flowers for a fast finishing touch. For more step-by-step techniques to accent brownies, visit www.wilton.com or see the Wilton Yearbook of Cake Decorating.

Star

The star is one of the easiest decorations to master—essential for filling in outlined areas and borders.

Icing Consistency: Medium

Bag Position: 90° (straight up)

Hold Tip: Between ⅛ and ¼ in. above surface

1. Hold bag in position with one hand while your other hand holds the tip steady. Squeeze bag to form a star. Increasing or decreasing the pressure changes the size of the star.

2. Stop squeezing the bag completely before you lift the tip from the star.

3. Lift the tip up and pull away from piped star.

Shell

The most popular icing technique of all, the shell is the basis for many borders. Lift the tip only slightly when piping shells to avoid a bumpy look.

Icing Consistency: Medium

Bag Position: 45° at 6:00

Hold Tip: Slightly above surface

1. Hold the bag in the 6:00 position so that you can pull the bag toward you. The tip should be slightly above the surface.

2. Squeeze hard, letting the icing fan out generously as it lifts the tip—do not lift the bag. Gradually relax your pressure as you lower the tip until it touches the surface.

3. Stop pressure and pull the tip away, without lifting it off the surface, to draw it to a point. To make a border, start the end of your next shell so that the fanned end covers the tail of the preceding shell to form an even chain.

Bead

A pretty border decoration, which uses a shell motion. To make a bead heart, pipe one bead, then a second, joining the tails. Smooth together using a decorator brush.

Icing Consistency: Medium

Bag Position: 45° at 3:00 (9:00 for lefties)

Hold Tip: Slightly above surface

1. Squeeze as you lift tip slightly so that icing fans out.

2. Relax pressure as you draw the tip down and bring bead to a point.

3. To make a bead border, start the end of your next bead so that the fanned end covers the tail of the preceding bead to form an even chain.

Rosette

These are ideal candle holders; just pipe and position your candle in the center. They also look great finished with a center star or dot.

Icing Consistency: Medium

Bag Position: 90° (straight up)

Hold Tip: Lightly touching surface

1. Keeping the tip slightly above the surface, squeeze out icing to form a star and, without releasing pressure, move the tip in a tight, complete rotation, starting at 9:00 (3:00) moving to 12:00...

2. then to 3:00 (9:00) and 6:00...

3. and ending back at 9:00 (3:00).

4. Stop pressure and lift tip up and away.

The Wilton Rose

NOTE: If you are going to be placing your roses on your cake immediately, waxed paper squares are not needed. To remove finished roses, use the Wilton Flower Lifter. Slide flower from lifter onto treat, using a spatula.

Icing Consistency: Royal or Stiff Buttercream

Bag Position: Base 90° (straight up); petals 45° at 4:30 (7:30)

Hold Tip: For base, slightly above nail; for petals, wide end touching base

Flower Nail: #7

1. Make the rose base, using tip 12 and flower nail #7. Hold the bag straight up, the end of tip 12 slightly above the center of your waxed paper-covered flower nail, which is held in your other hand. Using heavy pressure, build up a base, remembering to keep your tip buried as you squeeze. Start to lift the tip higher,

gradually raise the tip, and decrease the pressure.

2. Stop pressure, pull up and lift away. The rose base should be 1½ times as high as the rose tip opening.

3. Make the center bud, using tip 104. Hold nail containing base in your left (right) hand and bag with rose

tip 104 in right (left) hand. Bag should be at a 45° angle to the flat surface of the nail and in the 4:30 (7:30) position. The wide end of the tip should touch the cone of the icing base at or slightly below the midpoint, and the narrow end of the tip should point up and angled over top of base.

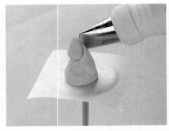

4. Now you must do 3 things at the same time: squeeze the bag, move the tip and rotate the nail. As you squeeze the bag, move the tip up from the base, forming a ribbon of icing. Slowly turn the nail counter-clockwise (clockwise for lefties) to

bring the ribbon of icing around to overlap at the top of the mound, then back down to starting point. Move your tip straight up and down only; do not loop it around the base.

5. Now you have a finished center bud.

6. Make the top row of 3 petals. Touch the wide end of tip to the midpoint of bud base, narrow end straight up.

7. Turn nail, keeping wide end of tip on base so that petal will attach. Move tip up and back down to the midpoint of mound, forming the first petal. (Rotate the nail ⅓ turn for each petal.)

8. Start again, slightly behind end of first petal, and squeeze out second petal. Repeat for the third petal, ending by overlapping the starting point of the first petal.

9. Make the middle row of 5 petals. Touch the wide end of tip slightly below center of a petal in the top row. Angle the narrow end of tip out slightly more than you did for the top row of petals. Squeeze bag and turn nail moving tip up, then down, to form first petal.

10. Repeat for a total of 5 petals, rotating the nail ⅓ turn for each petal.

11. The last petal end should overlap the first's starting point.

12. Make the bottom row of 7 petals. Touch the wide end of tip below the center of a middle row petal, again angling the narrow end of tip out a little more. Squeeze bag and turn nail to end of fingers,

moving tip up, then down to form first petal.

13. Repeat for a total of 7 petals, rotating the nail ⅓ turn for each petal.

14. The last petal end should overlap the first's starting point.

15. Slip waxed paper and completed rose from nail. This is the completed Wilton Rose.

Swirl Drop Flowers

The swirled look adds a nice motion effect. You must squeeze and turn at the same time.

Icing Consistency: Medium or Royal Icing

Bag Position: 90° (straight up)

Hold Tip: For flower, lightly touching surface; for center, slightly above flower

1. Turn your wrist in toward you before piping. Hold bag straight up, just touching the surface. You will turn wrist a full twist, starting with the flat

of your knuckles at 3:00 (9:00 for left-handers). As you squeeze out the icing, slowly turn your hand, with knuckles ending at 12:00.

2. Stop squeezing and lift the tip away.

3. Make a tip 3 dot flower center, holding your bag straight up and keeping the tip buried as you squeeze. Stop squeezing, then pull your tip up and away.

Leaves

Icing Consistency: Thinned with Corn Syrup

Bag Position: 45° at 6:00

Hold Tip: Lightly touching surface; Wide opening parallel to surface

Basic Leaf—Tip 352

Veined Leaf—Tip 67

Large Leaf—Tip 366
Use large coupler

These three leaves are all made following the same sequence.

1. Squeeze hard to build up the base, and at the same time lift the tip slightly.

2. Relax pressure as you pull the tip toward you drawing the leaf to a point.

3. Stop squeezing and lift away.

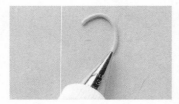

Ruffled Leaf

Squeeze, hold tip in place to let icing fan out into base, then move tip up and down to create ruffles. Relax, stop pressure and pull away.

Extended Leaf

Squeeze, move tip to desired length. Relax, stop pressure and pull tip away.

Stand-up Leaf

Touch tip lightly to surface and squeeze, holding tip in place as icing fans out to form base. Relax and stop pressure as you pull tip up and away.

Outline

Characters or designs are often outlined first, then piped in with stars or zigzags.

Icing Consistency: Thin

Bag Position: 45° at 3:00 (9:00)

Hold Tip: Slightly above surface

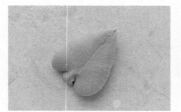

1. Touch tip to surface. Raise the tip slightly and continue to squeeze.

2. The icing will flow out of the tip while you direct it along the surface.

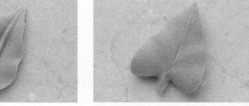

3. To end, stop squeezing, touch tip to surface and pull away.

Zigzag

A quick way to fill in outlined areas, great for ribbed sweater and cuff effects, hat brims and more.

Icing Consistency: Medium

Bag Position: 45° at 3:00 (9:00)

Hold Tip: Lightly touching surface

1. Steadily squeeze and move your hand in a tight up and down position.

2. Continue piping up and down with

steady pressure. To end, stop pressure and pull tip away. For more elongated zigzags, move your hand to the desired height while maintaining a steady pressure. For a more

relaxed look, increase the width as you move the bag along.

3. Repeat as you move in a straight line with consistent up/down motion.

Brownie Gallery

It doesn't take much to add a decorative touch! A brownie can be totally transformed with a fun-shaped cutter, a few well-placed sprinkles or tasty crunches, and exciting designs in Drizzle Icing or stenciled sugar. Think of these treats next time you need an easy but impressive dessert idea for a party. Find Wilton Brownie Products, including Crunches, Drizzle Icing, Brownie Stencil Set and more, starting on page 104.

Tasteful Gift
Top iced smooth with outline ribbon, bow and dot center.

Fruit Swirl
Spiral piped top with fresh raspberry and mint leaf.

All 'Round Fun
Top iced smooth and topped with Jumbo Confetti Sprinkles.

Heart Highlights
Top iced smooth with Pink Dusting Sugar heart and Confetti Sprinkles.

Butterfly Landing
Top iced smooth with butterfly stenciled in Blue Dusting Sugar.

Starburst Snacks
Top iced smooth with outline starburst and center piped star.

Candy Curl
Sides iced smooth and rolled in Chocolate Jimmies; topped with rosette and candy curl.

Neon Nibbles
Top iced smooth with outlines and Confetti Sprinkles.

A Name to Remember
Sides iced smooth, and rolled in Nonpareils; piped name.

Bolder Blossoms
Outlined petals dipped in Nonpareils with dot center.

Sweet Swirl
Top iced smooth and decorated with Peanut Butter Drizzle Icing spiral.

See the Rainbow
Top iced with zigzags and topped with Rainbow Chip Crunch.

Heart-Tugging Treat
Top iced smooth and decorated with Stylized Hearts (p. 11).

Brownies Go Nuts!
Sides iced smooth, rolled in Turtle Crunch and topped with rosette and sliced almond.

Party Star
Top iced smooth, with molded candy star and piped dots.

Diagonal Drama
Top iced smooth with Pink Dusted Sugar bands (mask open areas with parchment paper strips).

An Open Flower
Top iced smooth with petals piped in Vanilla Crème Drizzle Icing and Jumbo Confetti center.

Hint of Mint
Top iced smooth with Mint Drizzle Icing Feathered Lines (p. 11).

A Romantic at Heart
Top iced smooth and edged with Pink Cookie Icing scallops and center candy heart.

Minty Fresh
Edge outlined in icing and covered with Mint Crunch; topped with rosette and candy mint.

Dusted Daisy
Top iced smooth and covered with Pink Dusting Sugar and spice drop center.

Shower of Stars
Top iced smooth with Jumbo Stars Confetti.

Brownie Boutonniere!
Top iced smooth then combed with zigzag motion and topped with Wilton Rose.

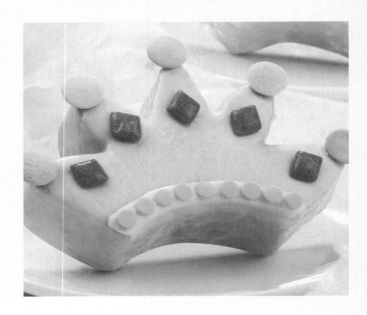

Kid Pleasers!

Serving brownies at the birthday party is an idea whose time has come—and the kids will agree!

As you're about to see, brownies look great decorated in a rainbow of colors from primaries to pastels. And just like a birthday cake, brownies can take on just about any shape. You can build fun designs on the classic square or rectangle, like a sailboat or 3-D birthday candles. Or use shaped bakeware and cookie cutters to create brownie bears, frogs, flowers and more.

Brownies can also stand in for other favorite kids party treats. They'll go wild over our brownie pops, dipped in colorful candy and sprinkles. You can even serve an entire brownie buffet, with everything from burgers and pizza to ice cream bars and 3-D cupcakes.

To add a little variety to the table, look for a great selection of fun mini treat ideas inside. We've covered several designs with candy, poured icing or ganache, which makes it easy to use cake or brownie batter as you like.

Delicious Wishes!

Pan:	13 x 9 x 2 in. Oblong Cake
Tips:	5, 16
Colors:	Rose, Lemon Yellow, Royal Blue, Kelly Green
Recipe:	Buttercream Icing, p. 103
Also:	Brownie Fudge Icing, Circle Metal Cutter, Rainbow Nonpareils Sprinkle Decorations, Assorted Wilton Celebration Candles

Bake and cool brownies in oblong pan; unmold. Cut circles using cutter. Sandwich 2 circles together with Fudge Icing. Ice top of stack with buttercream, spreading slightly over sides; sprinkle lightly with nonpareils. Pipe tip 5 wavy line at center of stack; add tip 5 ball bottom border. Pipe tip 16 rosette at top center; insert candle. Each serves 1.

Blowout Brownies!

Pan:	13 x 9 x 2 in. Oblong Cake
Tip:	2
Also:	Brownie Fudge Icing, Pink and Blue Dusting Sugars, Jumbo Confetti Sprinkle Decorations, Rolling Pin, Perfect Cut Brownie Cutter, Brownie Pop Sticks, Sugar Shaker, taffy (not salt water taffy), cardstock, scissors, waxed paper, plastic ruler, knife

Bake and cool 13 x 9 in. brownie. Score 1½ x 3 in. rectangles with Brownie Cutter, cut with knife. Ice brownies smooth with Fudge Icing. Attach jumbo confetti to some brownies with tip 2 dots of icing (trim some confetti to align with edge). For flames, cut lollipop stick to 3 in. Roll out taffy between waxed paper; cut flame shape with scissors. Insert lollipop stick in bottom of flame and insert into tops of candles. To decorate some brownies with Dusting Sugar just before serving, cut ⅜ in. wide cardstock strips, spray with nonstick pan spray and position diagonally over brownies. Dust between strips with Dusting Sugar in Sugar Shaker; carefully lift off cardstock. Each serves 1.

A Brownie Birthday Cake!

Pan: 8 x 2 in. Round (3)

Tip: 21

Recipe: Chocolate Buttercream Icing, p. 103

Also: Jumbo Confetti Sprinkle Decorations, Soft Colors Round Candles, malted milk balls, vanilla ice cream, plastic wrap

Bake and cool two 8 x 2 in. round brownies. Press ice cream into pan lined with plastic wrap; freeze to set. Unmold ice cream and stack between brownies. Ice "cake" smooth. Position malted milk balls for bottom border; position confetti sprinkles on cake sides. Pipe tip 21 rosette candleholders on top; freeze. Immediately before serving, insert candles. Serves 20.

Coast-to-Coast Fun

Pans: 13 x 9 x 2 in. Oblong Cake, Cooling Grid

Tips: 1, 1s, 4

Colors: * Royal Blue, Kelly Green, Lemon Yellow, Brown, Red-Red, Violet, Rose, Black, Copper

Recipe: Royal Icing, p. 103

Also: Round Comfort Grip Cutter, White Ready-To-Use Decorator Icing, Meringue Powder, Brownie Pop Sticks, large spice drops, round recessed candies, oval mini mints, knife, construction paper, cellophane tape

In advance: Make passengers and cars. For heads, using royal icing, pipe tip 1s dot facial features on round candies; let set. For car, cut spice drop horizontally in half; shape bottom into a rectangle with fingers. With tip 4, build up body and pipe pull-out arms. Add tip 1 outline fingers. Attach head to body with icing. Pipe tip 1 pull-out hair.

Also: Make flags. Cut triangles from paper. Tape to brownie pop sticks.

Bake and cool 1½ in. high cake in oblong pan, using firm-textured batter such as pound cake. Cut circles using round cutter; cut in half. Place treats on cooling grid over cookie sheet; cover with heated tinted icing (p. 12). Let set. Pipe tip 4 lines ¾ in. apart for grid-work on sides and track. Using royal icing, pipe tip 4 outlines for rails; attach mints. Using stiffened royal icing, pipe tip 4 outline top rail. Position cars. Cut sticks to desired lengths. Tape to serving plate or board. Each serves 1.

*Combine Brown with Red-Red for brown shown. Combine Violet with Rose for violet shown.

Circus Stars

Pans:	Silicone Mini Stars Mold, Cookie Sheet, Cooling Grid
Tips:	2, 13
Colors:	Lemon Yellow, Orange
Candy:	White, Orange or Light Cocoa Candy Melts, Garden Candy Color Set, Candy Melting Plate,
Recipe:	Buttercream Icing, p. 103
Also:	Jumbo Nonpareils Sprinkle Decorations, Parchment Triangles, Rolling Pin, Cake Boards, spice drops, waxed paper, granulated sugar, scissors

In advance: Make heads. Tint a portion of melted white candy to desired skin tone shade. For lighter colors, add a touch of orange to white candy, for brown, add a small amount of light cocoa to white candy. Pour into Candy Melting Plate cavities, filling ½ full; refrigerate until firm and unmold. Tint a portion of melted white candy black with candy color. Using tip 2 with a parchment bag, pipe eyes and mouth; let set.

Bake and cool star cakes or brownies in silicone mold supported by cookie sheet. Place treats on cooling grid over cookie sheet. Cover with melted candy (p. 12); refrigerate until firm. Attach candy head to top star point with melted candy. For hats, cut spice drops lengthwise in half with scissors. For hands and shoes, roll out spice drops on waxed paper sprinkled with sugar and cut shapes. Attach all with melted candy. Attach jumbo nonpareils for nose and buttons. In buttercream, pipe tip 13 zigzag trim and hair, rosette pompom. Each serves 1.

Pennant Fever!

Pans:	Silicone Mini Stars Mold, Cookie Sheet, Cooling Grid
Tip:	2
Colors:	Red-Red, Royal Blue
Also:	White Ready-To-Use Decorator Icing, Brownie Pop Sticks, gumballs, knife

Bake and cool cakes or brownies in silicone pan supported by cookie sheet. With knife, trim points off 2 side points to form flag cakes. Place treats on cooling grid over cookie sheet; cover with heated tinted icing (p. 12). Let set. Print tip 2 name using non-heated icing. For flag poles, insert stick in cake. Carefully cut hole in gumball; insert on stick. Each serves 1.

Fudgy Freeze

Pans: 13 x 9 x 2 in. Oblong Cake, Cooling Grid

Also: Light Cocoa Candy Melts, Rainbow Jimmies Sprinkle Decorations, Perfect Cut Brownie Cutter, Disposable Decorating Bags, Pastry Brush, knife, plastic ruler, ice cream sticks, waxed paper

Bake and cool brownies. Score 4 x 2 in. rectangles with brownie cutter; cut with knife. Insert ice cream stick in bottom. Position brownies on cooling grid above pan. Ice bottom side of brownie with melted candy; let set. Turn over; cover top and sides with melted candy in cut decorating bag. Sprinkle with jimmies and let set. Each serves 1.

Tasty Teddy

Pan: 9 x 9 x 2 in. Covered Brownie

Also: Brownie Fudge Icing, Teddy Bear Comfort Grip Cutter, Flowerful Medley Sprinkle Decorations, pink and green taffy (not salt water)

Bake and cool 9 in. square brownie. Cut bears using Comfort Grip cutter. Ice smooth with Fudge Icing. From sprinkle assortment, attach confetti eyes and nose and daisy buttons. Roll a small log of pink taffy, shape into mouth and attach. For bow tie, warm green taffy in hands and shape into triangle bows and ball knot; attach with Fudge Icing. Each serves 1.

Confetti Cupcakes

Pan: Dimensions Multi-Cavity Mini Cupcakes
Also: Brownie Fudge Icing, Spring Confetti Sprinkle Decorations, Pastry Brush, Brownie Gift Bag Kit

Bake and cool brownies in top and bottom pan sections. To attach cupcake sections, ice top of base smooth with Fudge Icing. Position cupcake top; ice smooth. Position confetti sprinkles. Let icing crust; place in gift bag. Each serves 1.

Lucky Numbers

Pan: 13 x 9 x 2 in. Oblong Cake

Also: Brownie Fudge Icing, Jumbo Confetti Sprinkle Decorations, Perfect Cut Brownie Cutter, knife, plastic ruler

Bake and cool 13 x 9 in. brownie; remove from pan. Score 4 x 2 in. rectangles with brownie cutter; cut with knife. Ice smooth with Fudge Icing. With spatula, score a line in center of brownie. Position jumbo confetti dots. Each serves 1.

One Sweet Pizza

Pan: Pizza Pan
Recipe: Brownie Pizza, p. 101
Also: Dark Cocoa Candy Melts, Parchment Triangles, mini marshmallows, candy-coated chocolates, chocolate chips, mini peanut butter cups (cut in pieces), knife

Bake and cool brownie in pizza pan. Top with marshmallows and candy. Drizzle with melted cocoa candy in cut parchment bag. Serves 12.

Brownie Burger

Pans: Mini Ball, 13 x 9 x 2 in. Oblong Cake
Tip: 5
Colors:* Orange, Golden Yellow, Lemon Yellow, Leaf Green, Red-Red
Recipes: Fudgy or Cake Brownies, p. 78; Blonde Brownies, p. 79; Buttercream Icing, p. 103
Also: Knife

Bake and cool blonde brownie buns in mini ball and chocolate brownie for patties ½ to ¾ in. high in 13 x 9 in. pan; remove from pan. Cut buns horizontally, cutting ⅓ off for bottom of bun with knife. Using mini ball cavity as pattern, cut chocolate brownie into round patties. Pipe tip 5 scallop lettuce on bottom bun half; position patty. Pipe tip 5 pull-out cheese and dot ketchup and mustard. Position top bun half. Each serves 1.

*Combine Orange with Golden Yellow for orange shown. Combine Golden Yellow with Lemon Yellow for yellow shown.

Big Brownie Bear

Pan:	Teddy Bear
Tip:	5
Colors:	Rose, Kelly Green
Recipe:	Buttercream Icing, p. 103

Also: Cake Board, Fanci-Foil Wrap, candy-coated chocolates, ⅝ in. wide satin ribbon (12 in.)

Bake and cool brownie, filling pan ⅓ deep; remove from pan. Position brownie on foil wrapped cake board that has been cut to the shape of the pan. Pipe tip 5 dot eyes and nose, outline mouth and number. Position chocolate pupils. Tie a ribbon bow and attach with dots of icing. Serves 12.

Treat the Whole Team!

Pan:	First and Ten Football
Tip:	18
Recipe:	Buttercream Icing, p. 103

Bake and cool brownie, filling pan ⅓ full; remove from pan. Pipe tip 18 zigzag stripes and outline stitching. Serves 12.

Petal Pickin'

Pan: 9 x 9 x 2 in. Covered Brownie

Also: Brownie Fudge Icing, Pink and Green Dusting Sugars, Oval, Leaf, Round Cut-Outs, Brownie Stencil Set, Nonpareils Sprinkle Decorations, Sugar Shaker, chocolate nougat candy, confectioners' sugar

Bake and cool 9 in. square brownie; unmold. Using Cut-Outs, cut 6 large oval petals, 1 medium round center and 1 large leaf for each flower. Ice petals, center and leaf smooth with Fudge Icing. Cover center with yellow nonpareils. For stem, knead four small chocolate nougat candies to form a rope. Just before serving, position stencils on petals and leaf; dust with Sugar Shaker (p. 11) Position stem and brownies. Each brownie serves 1.

Cute as a Bug

Pan:	Mini Ball
Tip:	2
Color:	Black
Recipe:	Buttercream Icing, p. 103
Also:	Jumbo Confetti Sprinkle Decorations, Light Cocoa Candy Melts, Disposable Decorating Bags, chocolate nougat candy, black shoestring licorice, green candy-coated chocolates, waxed paper, knife

Bake and cool mini ball brownies; remove from pan. Place several nougat candies on waxed paper; heat in microwave on very low power for 5 seconds. Roll a portion into a 1⅜ in. ball for head; flatten back. Shape and cut remaining nougat into ¾ in. high legs. Let all cool. Pipe tip 2 dot eyes and pupils, outline mouth. For antennae, cut 1 in. lengths of licorice; make holes in head with knife and insert. Secure with melted candy. Attach chocolates to antenna ends with melted candy. Attach head, feet and confetti spots to body with melted candy; refrigerate until firm. Each serves 1.

Hot Wings!

Pan:	9 x 9 x 2 in. Covered Brownie
Tips:	1, 7
Colors:	Rose, Leaf Green
Recipe:	Buttercream Icing, p. 103
Also:	Brownie Fudge Icing, Butterfly Comfort Grip Cutter, Flowerful Medley Sprinkle Decorations

Bake and cool 9 in. square brownie; unmold. Cut butterflies using Comfort Grip cutter. Ice smooth with Fudge Icing. Pipe tip 7 bead body and dot head with pink icing. Pipe tip 7 bead wing designs, tip 1 dot eyes and outline mouth. On wings, position yellow confetti from sprinkle assortment. Each serves 1.

Rolling Royally

Pans: 13 x 9 x 2 in. Oblong Cake, Cookie Sheet, Cooling Grid

Tips: 2, 4

Color: Rose

Also: Round Comfort Grip Cutter; White Ready-To-Use Decorator Icing, Jumbo Rainbow Nonpareils Sprinkle Decorations, Rolling Pin, large spice drops, vanilla wafers, granulated sugar, waxed paper, knife

Bake and cool 2 in. high cake or brownie; remove from pan. Cut circles using cutter. Heat Decorator Icing, tint and pour over treats (p. 12) and vanilla wafer wheels. Let set. Using non-heated icing, pipe tip 4 outline spokes and dot axles on wheels. Ice windows smooth. Pipe tip 2 outline windows and door on carriage. Attach nonpareils with dots of icing. Make crown. Roll out spice drop on waxed paper sprinkled with sugar. Cut crown shape with knife. Attach nonpareils with dots of icing. Attach wheels and crown with icing; support with spice drops if needed. Each serves 1.

Easy Bee

Pan: 13 x 9 x 2 in. Oblong Cake, Cooling Grid

Tips: 2, 5

Colors: Black, Lemon Yellow

Recipe: Buttercream Icing, p. 103

Also: Heart Combo Cutters, Yellow Candy Melts, mini candy-coated chocolates, black shoestring licorice

Bake and cool 2 in. high cake or brownies. Cut hearts using combo cutter. Cover treats with thinned buttercream (p. 12). Using full-strength icing, outline wing area with tip 5. Pipe tip 5 striped body. Attach a yellow Candy Melts wafer for head. Pipe tip 2 dot eyes, pupils, outline mouth. Cut 1¼ in. pieces of licorice; insert in cake. Attach mini chocolates with dots of icing. Each serves 1.

Her Highness' Hat

Pans: 13 x 9 x 2 in. Oblong Cake, Cookie Sheet, Cooling Grid

Candy: White Candy Melts, Garden Candy Color Set

Also: Jumbo Confetti, Jumbo Diamonds, Spring Confetti Sprinkle Decorations, Red Sparkle Gel, Daisy Comfort Grip Cutter, Circle Metal Cutter, Parchment Triangles, Cake Boards, knife, waxed paper, tweezers

In advance: Prepare diamonds. Place diamond sprinkles on waxed paper; pipe with Sparkle Gel. Let dry.

Bake and cool 1 in. high brownie or cake in oblong pan; remove from pan. Cut daisy shapes with Comfort Grip cutter. Using edge of circle cutter, cut daisy 2½ in. from top point for bottom curve of crown. Trim side points to create straight edge. Tint portions of melted candy pink using candy color. Ice

bottom of treats with melted candy; refrigerate until firm. Cover treats with melted candy (p. 12); refrigerate until firm. Using melted white candy in parchment bag, pipe band at bottom of crown; refrigerate until firm. Attach confetti sprinkles with dots of candy; let set. Pipe additional dots of melted candy to secure diamonds. Position diamonds using tweezers; let set. Each serves 1.

Rally Caps

Pans: Mini Ball, Non-Stick Cookie Sheet
Candy:* Red, Blue Candy Melts, Primary Candy Color Set
Also: 101 Cookie Cutters Set, Parchment Triangles, knife

In advance: Make candy brims. Position medium circle cutter from set on non-stick cookie sheet. Fill inside cutter ⅛ in. deep with melted Candy Melts. Refrigerate until firm; unmold. Repeat as needed, making one brim for each hat.

Bake and cool brownies; remove from pan. Using knife, trim to 1½ in. high. Position brownie cap on candy, covering about ½ of the circle. Pipe outline seams, letter and dot button using matching color melted candy; let set. Each serves 1.

*Add blue candy color to melted blue Candy Melts for blue shown.

I'd Lava Brownie!

Pans: Silicone Round Brownie Pops Mold, Cookie Sheet, Cooling Grid
Colors: Kelly Green, Lemon Yellow
Also: Cake Boards, Fanci-Foil Wrap, Brownie Pop Sticks, White Ready-To-Use Decorator Icing, Orange Tube Decorating Gel, shredded coconut, zip-close plastic bag, white cardstock, cellophane tape, fine-tip black marker

Bake and cool brownies in prepared Brownie Pops mold supported by cookie sheet. Unmold brownies; position on cooling grid. Tint a portion of icing yellow; heat to pouring consistency and pipe over top of brownie (p. 12). Overpipe with a little orange tube gel. Position brownie on foil-wrapped cake circle. Tint coconut green in plastic bag; position around brownie. From cardstock, cut a message cloud; print name with marker and tape to stick. Cut stick as needed and insert in brownie. Each serves 1.

Bake Sail

Pan:	9 x 9 x 2 in. Covered Brownie
Also:	Brownie Fudge Icing, Brownie Pop Sticks, Parchment Triangles, Perfect Cut Brownie Cutter, mini candy-coated chocolates, construction paper, cellophane tape, plastic ruler, knife

Bake and cool 9 in. square brownie. Score 4 x 2½ in. diamond shapes with Brownie Cutter; cut brownies with knife. Ice tops smooth with Fudge Icing. Position mini chocolates on edge. From paper, cut a 3 x 3 x 3 in. triangle sail; cut stick to desired height, tape sail to stick. Insert sail in brownie. Each serves 1.

First Down Brownie

Pan:	9 x 9 x 2 in. Covered Brownie
Tip:	5
Also:	Brownie Fudge Icing, White Ready-To-Use Decorator Icing, 101 Cookie Cutters Set

Bake and cool 9 in. square brownie; remove from pan. Cut shapes using football cutter from set. Ice brownies smooth with Fudge Icing. Outline tip 5 laces using white icing. Each serves 1.

Soccer Sensation

Pan:	9 x 9 x 2 in. Covered Brownie
Tips:	2, 16
Also:	Brownie Fudge Icing, White Ready-To-Use Decorator Icing, 101 Cookie Cutters Set

Bake and cool 9 in. square brownie; remove from pan. Cut circles using medium round cutter from set. Ice smooth with Fudge Icing. Pipe tip 2 outline sections of ball with white icing. Fill in some sections with tip 16 stars. Each serves 1.

Dino Mites!

Pans: Silicone Round Brownie Pops Mold, Cookie Sheet, Cooling Grid

Tips: 2, 5

Colors:* Leaf Green, Lemon Yellow, Orange, Pink, Black

Also: Ready-To-Use Decorator Icing, Blue Sparkle Gel, Rolling Pin, spice drops, taffy (not salt water), granulated sugar, shredded coconut, zip-close plastic bag, scissors, waxed paper, cornstarch, cardboard, foamcore or plywood board for serving

In advance: Make grass. Tint coconut green in plastic bag; let dry.

Bake and cool brownies in silicone mold supported by cookie sheet; unmold. Ice smooth. For head, roll a ¾ in. ball of taffy and attach with icing. For spikes, roll out spice drops on waxed paper sprinkled with sugar. Cut ½ in. high triangles with scissors; attach with icing. Pipe tip 5 outline legs and pull-out tail. Pipe tip 2 dot spots (flatten spots with finger dipped in cornstarch). Pipe tip 2 dot and string facial features. For pond, tape a cardboard square onto serving board; squeeze on Sparkle Gel. Position treats and grass. Each serves 1.

*Combine Leaf Green with Lemon Yellow for green shown.

Just a Little Jumpy!

Pans: Silicone Round Brownie Pops Mold, Cookie Sheet, Cooling Grid
Tips: 2, 5, 7
Colors: Red-Red, Leaf Green, Black
Also: White Ready-To-Use Decorator Icing

Bake and cool brownies in silicone mold supported by cookie sheet; unmold. Place treats on cooling grid; Cover with heated, tinted Decorator Icing (p. 12). Let set. Using unheated icing, pipe tip 7 legs and ball feet on sides, tip 5 legs and dot toes in front. Pipe tip 5 ball eyelids; overpipe for dimension. Pipe tip 5 whites of eyes. Pipe tip 2 dot pupils, nostrils. Outline and pipe in mouth with tip 2; add bead tongue. Each serves 1.

Built for Speed

Pans: Silicone Blossom Brownie Pops Mold, Cookie Sheet, Cooling Grid
Tips: 1A, 2, 12
Colors: Leaf Green, Black
Also: White Ready-To-Use Decorator Icing, cornstarch

Bake and cool brownies in silicone mold supported by cookie sheet; unmold. Trim bottoms for ¾ in. high treats. Place treats on cooling grid; cover with heated decorator icing (p. 12). Let set. Using unheated icing, pipe in tip 1A shell; pipe tip 1A ball head. Pipe in legs and spots with tip 12 (flatten and smooth spots with finger dipped in cornstarch); add pull-out tail. Pipe tip 2 dot eyes, toes and outline mouth. Each serves 1.

Monkeys Shine!

Pan:	Standard Muffin
Tips:	2, 5
Color:	Black
Also:	Brownie Fudge Icing, White Ready-To-Use Decorator Icing, Light Cocoa Candy Melts, White Standard Baking Cups, cornstarch

Bake and cool cupcakes; ice smooth with Fudge Icing. For ears, Insert 2 Candy Melts wafers. Tint a small amount of Fudge Icing with white icing to lighten. Pipe in snout and inside ears with tip 5 (pat smooth with finger dipped in cornstarch). Tint another portion of Fudge Icing black. Pipe tip 2 dot eyes, nose and outline mouth. Each serves 1.

Grab a Lion's Share

Pan:	Silicone Blossom Brownie Pops Mold
Tips:	2, 5, 7
Colors:*	Orange, Golden Yellow, Lemon Yellow, Brown
Recipe:	Buttercream Icing, p. 103; Favorite crisped rice cereal treats
Also:	Candy-coated chocolates, shredded coconut, zip-close plastic bag, cornstarch

Prepare cereal treats; press into mold cavities and immediately unmold. Tint coconut orange in plastic bag; let dry. Pipe in tip 7 head (smooth with finger dipped in cornstarch). Pipe tip 5 tear drop-shaped snout (flatten and smooth), tip 2 dot eyes and outline mouth. Using tip 2, pipe zigzag around head and position coconut for mane. Position candy-coated chocolates for ears. Each serves 1.

*Combine Golden Yellow with Lemon Yellow for yellow shown.

Bengal Buddy

Pan: Standard Muffin
Tips: 2, 5, 7
Color: Orange, Black
Recipe: Buttercream Icing, p. 103
Also: Brownie Fudge Icing, Orange Candy Melts, White Standard Baking Cups, knife, cornstarch

Bake and cool cupcakes; ice smooth in buttercream. For ears, insert 2 Candy Melts wafers in cupcake. Pipe in inner ears with tip 5 (smooth with finger dipped in cornstarch). Pipe in teardrop-shaped snout with tip 7. Pipe in nose and outline mouth with tip 2. Using Fudge Icing, pipe in tip 2 stripes. Each serves 1.

Laughing Giraffe

Pan: Standard Muffin
Tips: 2, 5
Colors: Golden Yellow, Lemon Yellow, Red-Red
Recipe: Buttercream Icing, p. 103
Also: Yellow Candy Melts, White Standard Baking Cups, Jumbo Confetti Sprinkle Decorations, pretzel sticks, mini candy-coated chocolates, cornstarch, knife

Bake and cool cupcakes; ice smooth. Pipe tip 5 ball snout; (flatten and smooth with finger dipped in cornstarch). Pipe tip 2 dot nostrils; outline and pipe-in mouth. For ears, cut teardrop shapes from a Candy Melts wafer; insert in cupcake. Position candy-coated mini chocolate eyes. For horns, insert pretzel sticks; attach confetti with dots of icing. Each serves 1.

Space Cadets

Pans: Silicone Round Brownie Pops Mold, Cookie Sheet, Cooling Grid

Candy: White, Yellow Candy Melts; Garden Candy Color Set; Stars Candy Mold

Also: 6 in. Cake Circle, Fanci-Foil Wrap, Parchment Triangles, Brownie Pop Sticks, 6 x 2 in. craft circle, Rolling Pin, knife, jelly spearmint leaves, gumballs, purple curling ribbon, 2 in. wide black ribbon (19"), waxed paper, kitchen towels, straight pins, scissors, granulated sugar, cellophane tape

In advance: Make 9 star candies. Fill mold cavities with melted yellow candy; refrigerate until firm and unmold. Reserve remaining candy. **Also:** Prepare base. Place craft circle on 6 in. cake circle and wrap with foil; secure with tape. Secure black ribbon to side with pins. Attach candies to sides with melted candy.

Bake and cool brownies in prepared mold supported by cookie sheet; unmold. Tint small portions of melted white candy pink and black using candy colors; tint reserved yellow candy green. With spatula, ice bottoms of brownies with green candy; position on waxed paper-covered board. Refrigerate until firm; remove paper. Cover brownies with melted green candy (p. 12); refrigerate until firm. Using knife, poke a small hole at top of brownie; insert Brownie Pop stick through entire brownie. Remove stick. Cut spearmint leaves horizontally in thirds with scissors. Attach 2 to bottom with melted candy for feet, leaving hole open; let set. Roll out remaining thirds on waxed paper sprinkled with sugar. Cut ears with knife; attach with melted candy. Refrigerate until firm. Re-insert stick, extending ½ in. at top; secure at top and bottom with melted candy.

Let set on gathered towels to keep stable. While still on towels, pipe dot eyes, pupils, nose, zigzag mouth and bead tongue using melted candy in cut parchment bags; let set. With knife, cut hole in gumball; insert on stick. Insert brownies in base. Position curling ribbon. Each brownie serves 1.

Day Brightening Bouquet

Pan:	Silicone Blossom Brownie Pops Mold
Tip:	5
Colors:*	Rose, Sky Blue, Violet, Lemon Yellow,
Recipe:	Buttercream Icing, p. 103
Also:	Jumbo Confetti Sprinkle Decorations, Brownie Pop Sticks, jelly spearmint leaves, craft foam, 5 in. flower pot or container, knife, scissors, curling ribbon

Bake and cool brownies in mold supported by cookie sheet; unmold and trim to level. Outline petals with tip 5 in rose, blue, violet and yellow buttercream. Insert sticks. Cut a small slit in spearmint leaf and slide onto stick. Attach confetti for flower center with a dot of icing. Position craft foam, cut to fit, inside container.

Insert brownies on sticks in container. Curl ribbon and arrange around sticks. Each brownie serves 1.

*Combine Violet with Rose for violet shown.

Pop Into the Party!

Pans:	Silicone Round Brownie Pops Mold, Mini Muffin, Cookie Sheet, Cooling Grid
Candy:	White Candy Melts, Primary and Garden Candy Color Sets, Brownie Pop Sticks
Also:	White Sparkling Sugar, Light Green, Pink, Red, Lavender, Orange Colored Sugars, Fanci-Foil Wrap, Piping Gel, Parchment Triangles, Brush Set, 6 in. Cake Circle, candy buttons, white curling ribbon, 6 x 2 in. craft circle, plastic wrap, cellophane tape

Bake and cool cakes in Mini Muffin Pan and brownies in Brownie Pops Mold supported by cookie sheet; trim bottoms flat. Tint portions of melted white candy violet, green, orange, yellow, red and pink. For gumdrops, ice bottoms of brownies smooth with candy; refrigerate until firm. Cover with melted candy (p. 12); refrigerate until firm and repeat. Insert stick in bottom; secure with melted candy. Brush brownies with Piping Gel and dip in sparkling sugar. For wrapped candy cakes, repeat steps for icing and covering in candy; refrigerate until firm. Using melted candy in cut parchment bags, pipe swirls and pinwheels on cakes; refrigerate until firm. Brush design areas with Piping Gel and sprinkle with matching color sugar. Wrap cakes in plastic wrap, twisting on each side and securing with a small piece of ribbon. Insert stick.

For base, place craft circle on 6 in. cake circle and wrap with foil. Tape strips of candy buttons to sides. Insert treats, trimming some sticks as needed. Position curling ribbon. Each serves 1.

Fun Flower Faces

Pans:	13 x 9 x 2 in. Oblong Cake, Cooling Grid
Candy:	Light Cocoa and White Candy Melts, Primary and Garden Candy Color Sets, Candy Melting Plate
Recipe:	Favorite crisped rice cereal treats
Also:	Flower Comfort Grip Cutter, Brownie Pop Sticks, Parchment Triangles, Mini Treat Baskets, 3¼ x 1 in. high craft foam circle, hot glue gun, jelly spearmint leaves, curling ribbon

In advance: Make candy face. Tint portion of melted white candy yellow. Fill melting plate cavities with yellow candy; refrigerate until firm and unmold. Pipe dot eyes and outline mouth using melted cocoa candy in cut parchment bag; refrigerate until firm. **Also:** Make stands. Using glue gun, attach craft foam circle inside Mini Treat Basket.

Prepare cereal treats; press mixture into pan and unmold. Cut flowers using Comfort Grip cutter. Cover treats with melted cocoa candy (p. 12); let set. Turn treats over and repeat; let set. Tint portion of white candy pink. Outline petals using melted candy in cut parchment bag. Attach candy face to treat and spearmint leaf to stick using melted cocoa candy; let set. Insert treat in base. Position curling ribbon. Each serves 1.

Living in the Present!

Pans: Silicone Brownie Bites Mold, Cookie Sheet, Cooling Grid

Tip: 5

Colors: Orange, Red-Red, Lemon Yellow, Kelly Green

Candy: Yellow, Red, Light Cocoa, Blue, Green and White Candy Melts, Primary and Garden Candy Color Sets, Candy Melting Plate

Recipe: Buttercream Icing, p. 103

Also: Flowerful Medley Sprinkle Decorations, Parchment Triangles, Cake Boards, Rolling Pin, spice drops, waxed paper, granulated sugar, scissors

In advance: Make candy box lids. Fill silicone mold ⅛ in. deep with melted candy; refrigerate until firm and unmold. **Also:** Make candy heads. Tint a portion of melted white candy to desired skin tone shade. For lighter colors, add a touch of orange to white candy, for brown, add a small amount of light cocoa to white candy. Pour into Candy Melting Plate cavities, filling ½ full; refrigerate until firm and unmold. Tint a small amount of melted light cocoa candy black using candy color. Place heads on waxed paper covered cake board and pipe hair, eyes, noses and mouths using melted candy in a cut parchment bag. Let set.

Bake and cool cakes or brownies in silicone mold supported by cookie sheet; unmold. Trim tops level. For each treat, stack 2 treats and place cut sides together. Cover with melted candy (p. 12); refrigerate until firm. Using tip 5 and buttercream icing, pipe ribbon on sides of packages and on box lids. For bow, roll out spice drops on waxed paper sprinkled with sugar. Cut into ⅛ in. diameter ropes, 1¾ in. long. Pinch ends to form loops. Roll 1¼ in diameter ball for knot. Attach 4 loops and knot with dots of icing to lid.

Cut spice drop lengthwise in half to support head; attach with melted candy. Attach head to cake and lid to head with melted candy. Attach confetti from Flowerful Medley assortment to sides of boxes with dots of melted candy. Each serves 1.

Soda Celebration

Pan:	Silicone Round Brownie Pops Mold; Cookie Sheet
Tip:	2D
Colors:*	Rose, Lemon Yellow, Golden Yellow, Kelly Green
Candy:	White and Light Cocoa Candy Melts, Primary and Garden Candy Color Sets, Candy Melting Plate
Recipe:	Buttercream Icing, p. 103
Also:	Rainbow Jimmies Sprinkle Decorations, Parchment Triangles, sour cherry candies, pretzel sticks, waxed paper

In advance: Make candy bases. Fill melting plate cavities with melted cocoa candy; refrigerate until firm.
Also: Make straws. Dip pretzel sticks in melted white candy; let set on waxed paper. Tint melted white candy red, blue and orange using candy colors. Using melted candy in cut parchment bag, pipe lines around pretzels; let set.

Bake and cool brownies in mold supported by cookie sheet; unmold. Attach to bases with melted candy; let set. With buttercream, pipe tip 2D swirl on top; sprinkle with jimmies. Position cherry candy and pretzel straw. Each serves 1.

*Combine Lemon Yellow with Golden Yellow for yellow shown.

Happy Hats

Pan:	Silicone Round Brownie Pops Mold
Tip:	2
Colors:*	Rose, Lemon Yellow, Violet
Recipe:	Buttercream Icing, p. 103, favorite crisped rice cereal treats
Also:	Brownie Pop Sticks, Flowerful Medley Sprinkle Decorations, Disposable Decorating Bags

Prepare cereal treats and press into mold cavities; immediately unmold. Let set to firm up for at least 30 minutes. Insert sticks. Ice smooth, building up top of hats into points. Attach confetti from Flowerful Medley assortment with dots of icing. Pipe tip 2 pull-out dot trim. Each serves 1.

*Combine Violet with Rose for violet shown.

Parfait Perfection

Recipe:	Leftovers from any cut brownies
Also:	Rainbow Jimmies Sprinkle Decorations, Parchment Triangles, vanilla ice cream, hot fudge topping, maraschino cherries

Layer ice cream and brownie pieces in serving dish, ending with a layer of ice cream. Pipe warmed topping over top using cut parchment bag. Sprinkle with Rainbow Jimmies. Position cherry. Each serves 1.

Cone-verted Brownies

Tip:	21
Recipe:	Buttercream Icing, leftovers from any cut brownies
Also:	Rainbow Jimmies Sprinkle Decorations, Parchment Triangles, hot fudge topping, cake ice cream cones, maraschino cherries

Fill cone with brownie pieces shaping to form a rounded top. Top with tip 21 swirl of buttercream. Pipe warmed topping over top using cut parchment bag. Sprinkle with Rainbow Jimmies. Position cherry. Each serves 1.

A Worm Welcome

Pan: 9 x 9 x 2 in. Covered Brownie
Recipe: Quick Chocolate Mousse, p. 101
Also: Round Mini Treat Baskets, gummy worms, knife, zip-close plastic bag

Prepare mousse recipe. Bake and cool 9 in. square brownie; remove from pan. Using knife, cut brownie into small chunks; place in zip-close bag and knead with fingers to create small crumbs. Place a layer of crumbs in each basket; top with a layer of mousse, then a 2nd layer of crumbs. Position gummy worms. Each serves 1.

Fun-To-Do Fondue!

Pan: 9 x 9 x 2 in. Covered Brownie
Candy: Chocolate Pro Electric Melting Pot, Light Cocoa Candy Melts, Brownie Pop Sticks, Metal Dipping Set
Also: Rainbow Chip, Cookies & Cream, Turtle, Mint Brownie Crunches, Cake Boards, dipping bowls, waxed paper, knife

Bake and cool 9 in. square brownie; remove from pan. Cut brownies into 1 in. squares.

Melt Candy Melts in melting pot. Using dipping fork, dip squares in candy to coat completely. Tap lightly on edge of pot to remove excess. Place squares on waxed paper-covered board. Insert stick and refrigerate until firm. Holding by stick, dip top half of square in melted candy; tap to remove excess and immediately dip into crunches. Refrigerate until firm. Each serves 1.

Fun-Topped Pops

Pans: Silicone Round Brownie Pops Mold, Cookie Sheet, Cooling Grid

Also: Dark and Light Cocoa, White, Blue, Yellow, Orange, Pink, Green Candy Melts, Chocolate Jimmies, White Nonpareils, Rainbow Nonpareils Sprinkle Decorations, Turtle Brownie Crunch, Parchment Triangles, Cake Board, Brownie Pop Sticks, waxed paper

Bake and cool brownies in silicone mold supported by cookie sheet; unmold. Insert stick into rounded end for fully-dipped pops, flat end for partially-dipped pops. Dip pops in melted white or cocoa candy. Immediately dip partially-dipped pops in sprinkles or crunches. Let set on waxed paper-covered cake board. Drizzle fully-dipped pops with melted candy in cut parchment bag; let set. Each serves 1.

Seasons to Celebrate

Finding something new to serve at holiday get-togethers is always a challenge. We suggest an old favorite—brownies—presented in amazing shapes that are a fun surprise in any season!

You know that chocolate is welcome any time of year. The big news is that with all the ways to add festive color, brownies can be dressed up to create the perfect look for any seasonal celebration. With Sprinkles, candy, icing and Dusting Sugar, it's easy to serve treats that set the tone for the holiday.

If you want to be ready for an entire year of holiday treats, look to our Brownie Pops Mold. This silicone mold bakes the fun dome-shaped treats you'll see throughout this section—as Halloween bats, brooms and ghosts, North Pole penguins for Christmas, and stand-up Easter eggs and baskets. And because holidays mean gifting, we're also featuring terrific ways to present treats, including a window box filled with fudgy ornaments and a Valentine envelope with a heart-shaped brownie inside.

Heart Art

Pan: 9 x 9 x 2 in. Covered Brownie
Also: Heart Combo Cutter, Brownie Fudge Icing, Vanilla Crème Drizzle Icing, Pink Cookie Icing, toothpick

Bake and cool 9 in. square brownie; remove from pan. Cut brownies using Combo Cutter. Ice smooth with Fudge Icing. Heat Drizzle and Cookie Icings following package directions. Drizzle lines of white or pink icing across brownie; immediately drag toothpick through lines, alternating directions to form designs. Each serves 1.

We're Talking Chocolate

Pan: 9 x 9 x 2 in. Covered Brownie, Cookie Sheet, Cooling Grid
Candy: Light Cocoa and White Candy Melts, Primary and Garden Candy Color Sets
Also: 6 Pc. Valentine Mini Cutter Set, Parchment Triangles, Cake Board, Spatula, waxed paper

Bake and cool 9 in. square brownie; remove from pan. Cut brownies using smallest heart cutter from set. Cover with melted cocoa candy (p. 12); Refrigerate until firm. Tint portions of melted white candy yellow, violet, pink, green and orange using candy colors. Pipe message using melted candy in cut parchment bags; refrigerate until firm. Each serves 1.

Waves of Emotion

Pan: 9 x 9 x 2 in. Covered Brownie Pan

Also: Brownie Fudge Icing, Pink Cookie Icing, Vanilla Crème and Mint Drizzle Icings, Heart Comfort Grip Cutter, Brownie Envelope Kit, Heart Lollipop Mold, Light Cocoa Candy Melts, ribbon,

In advance: Make candy heart topper. Mold hearts using melted candy; refrigerate until firm and unmold. Bake and cool 9 in. square brownie; remove from pan; cut brownies using heart cutter. Ice smooth with Fudge Icing. Heat Drizzle and Cookie Icing following package directions. Pipe zigzag designs on hearts. Place brownie on envelope; fold flaps toward center and secure with seal. Attach candy heart with dot of melted candy. Each serves 1.

It's the Easter Brownie!

▪▪

Pan: 9 x 9 x 2 in. Covered Brownie
Tip: 5
Recipe: Buttercream Icing, p. 103
Color: Rose
Also: Brownie Fudge Icing, Bunny Face Comfort Grip Cutter, mini candy-coated chocolates, purple jelly beans, cornstarch

Bake and cool 9 in. square brownie; remove from pan. Cut bunny faces using cutter. Ice smooth with Fudge Icing. In buttercream icing, pipe in tip 5 eyes, ears, tongue and muzzle (pat smooth with finger dipped in cornstarch). Attach mini candy-coated chocolate pupils and jelly bean nose with dots of icing. Each serves 1.

Egg Hunt Prize

▪▪

Pan: 9 x 9 x 2 in. Covered Brownie
Also: Brownie Fudge Icing, Egg Comfort Grip Cutter, Spring Confetti Sprinkle Decorations, Blue and Pink Dusting Sugars, Sugar Shaker, waxed paper

Bake and cool 9 in. square brownie; remove from pan. Cut eggs using cutter. Ice smooth with Fudge Icing; let icing crust. Just before serving, cut 4 waxed paper strips to keep sections free from dusting sugar. Spray strips with non-stick cooking spray and position on brownie. Using shaker, dust stripes of pink and blue sugar; carefully remove strips. Attach confetti sprinkles with dots of icing. Each serves 1.

Fresh Eggs

Pan:	Silicone Round Brownie Pops Mold, Non-Stick Cookie Sheet
Tip:	2
Colors:*	Lemon Yellow, Violet, Rose, Leaf Green
Candy:	White Candy Melts, Garden Candy Color Set
Recipe:	Buttercream Icing, p. 103
Also:	Spring Confetti Sprinkle Decorations

In advance: Make candy bases. Tint melted Candy Melts green using candy color. On non-stick pan, pipe a 1¾ in. circle of green candy; refrigerate until firm.

Bake and cool brownies in Brownie Pops mold supported by cookie sheet (2 Brownie Pops needed for each treat). Unmold brownies and trim to 1¼ in. high. Pipe a small amount of melted candy on candy base; position 1 brownie, narrow end down, for bottom of egg; refrigerate until firm. Attach another brownie wide side down for top of egg with buttercream. Pipe 3 rows of tip 2 beads at center of egg. Attach confetti with dots of icing. Pipe tip 2 pull-out grass at base of egg. Each serves 1.

*Combine violet with rose for violet shown.

Goodie Basket

Pan:	Silicone Round Brownie Pops Mold, Non-Stick Cookie Sheet
Tips:	2, 7
Colors:	Leaf Green, Brown
Candy:	White Candy Melts, Garden Candy Color Set
Recipes:	Buttercream Icing, Royal Icing, p. 103
Also:	Meringue Powder, Disposable Decorating Bags, mini jelly beans, shredded coconut, waxed paper, zip-close plastic bag

In advance: On handle. On waxed paper, using royal icing, pipe a tip 7 outline handle for each treat, 1½ x 2 in. high; let dry overnight. **Also:** Make candy base. Tint melted Candy Melts green using candy color. On non-stick pan, pipe a 2 in. circle of green candy; refrigerate until firm. **And:** Tint coconut green in plastic bag; Let dry.

Bake and cool brownies in Brownie Pops mold supported by cookie sheet; unmold. Attach brownie and coconut to base with melted candy; refrigerate until firm. Using knife, cut 2 small holes in brownie top for handle position; insert handle. Pipe tip 2 pull-out grass on brownie top. Position mini jelly beans. Each serves 1.

Brownie Brew

Pan: 9 x 9 x 2 in. Covered Brownie
Tip: 5
Colors:* Lemon Yellow, Leaf Green
Also: Brownie Fudge Icing, White Ready-To-Use Decorator Icing, 18 Pc. Halloween Cutter Set, orange and yellow spice drops, pretzel sticks, waxed paper, scissors, granulated sugar, knife, rolling pin

Bake and cool 9 in. square brownie; remove from pan. Cut cauldron with cutter from set. Ice smooth with Fudge Icing. Pipe tip 5 dot bubbles. For flames, roll out spice drops on waxed paper sprinkled with sugar; cut flames with scissors. Attach to brownie with icing. Insert pretzel stick. Each serves 1.

*Combine Lemon Yellow with Leaf Green for green shown.

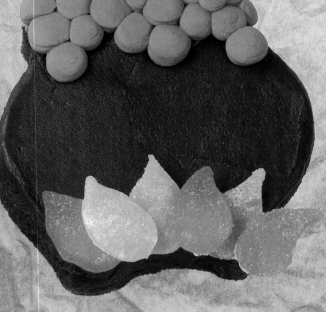

The Witch's Hat

Pan: 9 x 9 x 2 in. Covered Brownie
Tip: 5
Colors:* Lemon Yellow, Golden Yellow, Orange
Also: Brownie Fudge Icing, White Ready-To-Use Decorator Icing, Witch's Hat Comfort Grip Cutter, cornstarch

Bake and cool 9 in. square brownie; remove from pan. Cut hat using cutter. Ice smooth with Fudge Icing. Pipe tip 5 outline band (smooth with finger dipped in cornstarch). Add tip 5 outline buckle. Each serves 1.

*Combine Lemon Yellow with Golden Yellow for yellow shown.

Cocoa Coffin

Pan: 9 x 9 x 2 in. Covered Brownie
Tip: 2
Also: Brownie Fudge Icing, Orange Tube Decorating Icing, Coupler Ring Set, 18 Pc. Halloween Cutter Set

Bake and cool 9 in. square brownie; remove from pan. Cut coffin using coffin cutter from set. Ice smooth with Fudge Icing. Pipe tip 2 message. Each serves 1.

Broomin' Brownie

Pan:	Silicone Round Brownie Pops Mold, Cookie Sheet
Tips:	16
Color:	Golden Yellow
Also:	White Ready-To-Use Decorator Icing, Cake Boards, Fanci-Foil Wrap, jelly rings, pretzel rods, knife

Bake and cool brownies in Brownie Pops pan supported by cookie sheet. With knife, trim pretzel rod to approximately 5 in.; insert in top of brownie. With yellow tinted icing, pipe tip 16 outline bristles, starting from bottom and ending at top of brownie. Pipe tip 16 shell neck above brownie. For binding, cut jelly ring halves and position around neck. Each serves 1.

Wacky Webspinner

Pan:	Mini Ball
Tips:	2, 5
Color:	Black
Also:	White Ready-To-Use Decorator Icing, pretzel sticks, mini candy-coated chocolates, chocolate nougat candy

Bake and cool brownies; remove from pan. Pipe tip 5 dot eyes; attach mini candy-coated chocolate pupils and nose. Pipe tip 2 outline mouth and pull-out fangs. Insert pretzel sticks for upper portion of legs. Insert nougat on stick; insert pretzel sticks for ends of legs. Each serves 1.

Brownies Go Batty

Pan:	Silicone Round Brownie Pops Mold, Non-Stick Cookie Sheet
Tips:	2, 5
Colors:*	Leaf Green, Lemon Yellow, Black
Also:	White Ready-To-Use Decorator Icing, Light Cocoa Candy Melts, 9 Pc. Leaves and Acorns Nesting Cutter Set, rolling pin, knife, mini candy-coated chocolates, chocolate nougat candy, cornstarch

Bake and cool brownies in silicone mold supported by cookie sheet; unmold. Trim bottom flat with knife. For wings, place smallest oak leaf cutter from set on non-stick pan; fill inside of cutter ⅛ in. thick with melted cocoa candy. Refrigerate until firm. For ears, roll out nougat candy ⅛ in. thick; cut ½ in. triangles. Cut small slits on sides of bat for wings with knife. Insert wings; secure with melted candy. Attach ears with melted candy; refrigerate until firm. In buttercream, pipe tip 5 dot eyes and pupils (pat smooth with finger dipped in cornstarch). Using tip 2, outline mouth and fangs. Attach candy-coated chocolate nose with dot of icing. Each serves 1.

*Combine Leaf Green with Lemon Yellow for green shown.

Halloween Scene

Pan:	9 x 9 x 2 in. Covered Brownie, Silicone Round Brownie Pops Mold, Cookie Sheet, Cooling Grid
Tips:	2, 5, 7
Colors:*	Lemon Yellow, Leaf Green, Black, Orange
Recipe:	Buttercream Icing, p. 103
Also:	Brownie Fudge Icing, White Candy Melts, 18 Pc. Halloween Cutter Set, 10 in. Cake Circle, Fanci-Foil Wrap, Brownie Pop Sticks, 6 x 2 in. craft foam circle, green curling ribbon, shredded coconut, zip-close plastic bag, waxed paper, knife

In advance: Prepare base. Wrap craft circle and 10 in. cake circle in foil. Attach craft circle to 10 in. circle with melted candy; let set. **Also:** Tint coconut. Place in zip-close bag, add a few drops of green icing color and knead until color is evenly blended. Let dry on waxed paper.

Bake and cool ghost brownies in silicone mold supported by cookie sheet; unmold. With knife, trim bottom flat. Ice bottoms smooth with melted white candy; let dry on side. Cover brownies with melted white candy (p. 12); let set then repeat. In buttercream, pipe tip 7 dot eyes and pupils, tip 2 dot or zigzag mouths and outline eyebrows. Using tip of knife, make a small hole in bottom of ghost for stick. Then insert stick and set aside.

Bake and cool 9 in. square brownie; remove from pan. Cut 7 tombstones using cutter from set. Using tip 7, outline with Fudge Icing; using tip 5, add RIP in buttercream. Attach to base with icing. Cut sticks to various lengths and insert ghosts in base. Position curling ribbon and shredded coconut. Each brownie serves 1.

*Combine Leaf Green with Lemon Yellow for green shown.

Good Things in Small Packages

Pan:	9 x 9 x 2 in. Covered Brownie
Tip:	5
Colors:*	Red-Red, Christmas Red, Kelly Green, Royal Blue
Recipe:	Buttercream Icing, p. 103
Also:	Brownie Fudge Icing, Flowerful Medley Sprinkle Decorations, 18 Pc. Holiday Cutter Set, toothpick

Bake and cool 9 in. square brownie; remove from pan. Cut gifts using cutter from set. Ice smooth with Fudge Icing. In buttercream, pipe in tip 5 bow and outline ribbon. Score crease lines in bow with toothpick. Position matching color confetti dots from Flowerful Medley assortment. Each serves 1.

*Combine Red-Red with Christmas Red for red shown.

Party Penguins

Pan:	Silicone Round Brownie Pops Mold, Cookie Sheet, Cooling Grid
Tips:	2, 4
Colors:	Lemon Yellow, Black
Recipe:	Buttercream Icing, p. 103
Also:	Light Cocoa Candy Melts, spice drops, chocolate nougat candies, knife, cornstarch, rolling pin, granulated sugar, waxed paper

Bake and cool brownies in silicone mold supported by cookie sheet; unmold. With knife, trim bottom flat. Cover brownies with melted cocoa candy (p. 12); let set. Using buttercream, pipe tip 4 outline and pipe-in tummy (pat smooth with finger dipped in cornstarch). Pipe tip 2 dot eyes and pull-out beak. For wings, flatten nougat candies and cut teardrop shapes with knife; attach with melted candy. For feet, roll out yellow spice drops on waxed paper sprinkled with sugar; cut shapes with knife. Attach to bottom of brownies with candy. For hat, shape spice drops into a cone; attach with candy. Pipe tip 2 dots and pull-out fringe on hat. Each serves 1.

Brownie Blizzard

Pan:	9 x 9 x 2 in. Covered Brownie
Tip:	5
Recipe:	Buttercream Icing, p. 103
Also:	18 Pc. Holiday Cutter Set, Blue Dusting Sugar, Sugar Shaker

Bake and cool 9 in. square brownie; remove from pan. Cut snowflakes using cutter from set. Using Sugar Shaker sprinkle top with Blue Dusting Sugar. Using tip 5, pipe lines; add dot center. Each serves 1.

Treats for the Tree

Pan:	9 x 9 in. Covered Brownie
Tips:	5
Colors:*	Red-Red, Christmas Red, Kelly Green
Recipe:	Buttercream Icing, p. 103
Also:	Brownie Fudge Icing, Circle Metal Cutter, Brownie Gift Box Kit, mini candy-coated chocolates, marshmallows, cornstarch

Bake and cool 9 in. square brownie; remove from pan. Cut round ornaments using circle cutter. Ice smooth with Fudge Icing. In buttercream, pipe tip 5 outline stripe across brownie (pat smooth with finger dipped in cornstarch). Attach mini candy-coated chocolates. Cut marshmallow in half; attach at top with dots of icing. Position ornaments in box. Each serves 1.

*Combine Red-Red with Christmas Red for red shown.

The Beauty of Brownies!

Brownies are perfectly suited to be your special event's signature dessert. With their decadent flavor and no-fuss preparation, brownies are the ideal candidate for creating sophisticated single servings. On the following pages, we've given brownies the higher profile they deserve.

Look at the magic a few simple presentation touches can make! Finish off an iced or glazed brownie with a candy topper—bows, swirls or monograms will look great at a shower or anniversary celebration. Give basic brownies a color update with pastel icing flowers or stencil designs dusted with sugar. Or pair brownies with fruit and ice cream for an even more indulgent taste treat.

There are also bigger brownies to serve a crowd. For chocolate thrills, it's hard to beat the tall 3-layer torte crowned with candy scrolls. There's even a cheesecake makeover to wow your guests, with a rich brownie crust and fudge swirls and shells. What a way to finish the party!

Artistic Accents

Pan: 9 x 9 x 2 in. Covered Brownie

Candy: Light Cocoa Candy Melts; Candy Melting Plate

Also: Brownie Stencil Set; Pink Dusting Sugar; Brownie Fudge Icing; Sugar Shaker

In advance: Make candy dots. Fill melting tray cavities ¼ in. deep with melted cocoa candy; refrigerate until firm and unmold.

Bake and cool 9 in. square brownie; remove from pan. Ice smooth with Fudge Icing; let icing crust. Just before serving, position stencil on brownie and sprinkle design areas with dusting sugar (p. 11); carefully remove stencil. Position on serving plate. Position candy dots around brownie. Serves 20.

Stenciled Sensations

Pan: 9 x 9 x 2 in. Covered Brownie

Also: Brownie Fudge Icing, Pink and Green Dusting Sugars, Brownie Stencil Set, Sugar Shaker, plastic ruler, knife

Bake and cool 9 in. square brownie; remove from pan. Ice smooth with Fudge Icing; let icing crust. Cut into 2 x 3 in. rectangles. Just before serving, position stencil on brownie and sprinkle design areas with dusting sugars (p. 11); carefully remove stencil. Each serves 1.

Petite Florals

Pan: 9 x 9 x 2 in. Covered Brownie

Tip: 5

Also: Brownie Fudge Icing, Pink and Blue Dusting Sugars, Brownie Stencil Set, Round and Oval Cut-Outs, Flowerful Medley Sprinkle Decorations, Sugar Shaker, paper, cellophane tape

Bake and cool 9 in. square brownie; remove from pan. Cut shapes using large oval and round Cut-Outs. Pipe Fudge Icing over tops with tip 5; smooth with spatula. Let icing crust. On flower stencil, tape paper over other stencil areas so that only flower shows through. Just before serving, position stencil on brownie and sprinkle design areas with dusting sugars (p. 11); carefully remove stencil. Position yellow confetti from Flowerful Medley assortment for flower centers. Each serves 1.

Raspberry Romance

Pans: Dimensions 6-Cavity Mini Heart, Cooling Grid,

Also: Brownie Fudge Icing, Disposable Decorating Bags, fresh raspberries, fresh mint leaves

Bake and cool brownies in pan cavities; unmold. Position brownie on plate. Heat Fudge Icing following package directions to make a ganache; fill center cavity using a cut disposable bag. Position berries and mint. Each serves 1.

Brrrr-ownie Sandwiches

Pan: 13 x 9 x 2 in. Oblong Cake

Also: Round Comfort Grip Cutter, White Jumbo Baking Cups, assorted ice cream, knife, plastic wrap

Bake and cool brownie in oblong pan; remove from pan. For each sandwich, cut 2 round brownies using cutter. With knife, cut ice cream into 1 in. thick slices; cut rounds with cutter. Sandwich ice cream between brownies. Wrap in plastic wrap and freeze until ready to serve. Remove wrap and place in baking cups to serve. Each serves 1.

Sundae in a Shell

Pan: 6-Cavity Brownie Dessert Shell

Tip: 2D

Also: Vanilla Whipped Icing Mix, favorite ice cream, ice cream toppings, nuts, bananas, raspberries, maraschino cherries, mint leaves

Bake and cool brownies in shell pan; remove from pan. Position a scoop of ice cream in center. Add toppings, whipped icing, fruit and nuts. For whipped topping use tip 2D for star or rosette (p.13). Each serves 1.

Stirring Swirls Cheesecake

Pan:	9 x 3 in. Springform
Tips:	5, 21
Recipe:	Brownie Cheesecake, p. 82
Also:	Chocolate Ready-To-Use Decorator Icing, Cake Board, Fanci-Foil Wrap

Bake and cool brownie cheesecake in spring-form pan following recipe directions; unmold. Pipe tip 5 swirls on top in Decorator Icing. Pipe tip 21 rosette top border. Serves 12.

Twirling Torte

Pan: 13 x 9 x 2 in. Oblong Cake

Tips: 5, 21

Also: Chocolate Ready-To-Use Decorator Icing, Light Cocoa Candy Melts, Decorating Triangle, Parchment Triangles, Cake Board, Fanci-Foil Wrap, Brownie Pop Sticks, waxed paper, plastic ruler

In advance: Make candy swirls. On waxed paper-covered board, using melted candy in parchment bag fitted with tip 5, pipe 30 swirls, 1½ in. wide, with tails extending down 1½ in. long. Refrigerate until firm. Make extras to allow for breakage. Turn swirls over; repeat on back and refrigerate.

Bake and cool brownies in oblong pan; remove from pan. Cut into 3 sections, 9 x 4 in. each. Stack sections, filling and icing smooth with Decorator Icing. Comb sides with narrow-tooth edge of Decorating Triangle. Pipe tip 21 rosettes on top. Using sticks, make holes in top for insertion of candy swirls; insert swirls. Serves 15.

Knock Them for a Loop!

Pan: 9 x 9 x 2 in. Covered Brownie

Tip: 5

Color: Rose

Recipe: Buttercream Icing, p. 103

Also: Brownie Fudge Icing, Perfect Cut Brownie Cutter, knife, plastic ruler

Bake and cool 9 in. square brownie; remove from pan. Score 2½ in. squares using brownie cutter; cut with knife. Ice smooth with Fudge Icing. Pipe tip 5 swirls with buttercream or Fudge Icing. Each serves 1.

Sunny Brownies

Pan:	9 x 9 x 2 in. Covered Brownie
Tips:	2D, 2, 352
Colors:*	Lemon Yellow, Golden Yellow, Rose, Violet
Recipe:	Royal Icing, p. 103
Also:	Brownie Fudge Icing, Leaf Green Tube Decorating Icing, Coupler Ring Set, Mini Combo Cutter, Meringue Powder, Cake Board, Parchment Triangles, waxed paper

In advance: Make drop flowers. Using royal icing, on waxed paper-covered board, pipe one tip 2D drop flower for each treat. Add tip 2 dot centers. Let dry overnight.

Bake and cool 9 in. square brownie. Cut brownies using combo cutter. Ice smooth with Fudge Icing. Position flowers. Using tube icing, pipe tip 352 leaves. Each serves 1.

*Combine Lemon Yellow with Golden Yellow for yellow shown. Combine Violet with Rose for violet shown.

On A Softer Side

Pans:	Standard Muffin, Cooling Grid
Tips:	7, 103
Colors:	Rose, Lemon Yellow
Recipe:	Buttercream Icing, p. 103
Also:	Flower Nail No. 7, White Nonpareils Sprinkle Decorations, White Ready-To-Use Decorator Icing, Disposable Decorating Bags, waxed paper

Bake and cool brownies. Position brownie upside down on cooling grid; using heated icing in cut disposable bag, pipe over top of brownie (p. 12), letting icing drip down the sides. Sprinkle immediately with nonpareils. In buttercream, make a tip 103 rose with tip 7 base for each treat. Position rose. Each serves 1.

Flowers Unfurled

Pan:	13 x 9 x 2 in. Oblong Cake
Tip:	5
Colors:	Royal Blue, Lemon Yellow, Rose
Recipe:	Buttercream Icing, p. 103
Also:	Brownie Fudge Icing, Yellow, Pink and Blue Candy Melts, Round Cut-Outs, 13 Count Standard Cupcakes 'N More Dessert Stand, Parchment Triangles, Cake Boards, White Mini Baking Cups, waxed paper

In advance: Make candy loop petals. Using melted candy in cut parchment bag, pipe 11 loops ¾ in. high x ½ in. wide for each flower on waxed paper-covered board. Make extras to allow for breakage; refrigerate until firm.

Bake and cool brownies in oblong pan; remove from pan. Cut circles using largest round Cut-Out. Ice brownies smooth with Fudge Icing. Using buttercream, pipe tip 5 ball in center of brownie; insert loop petals to form flower. Position brownies on flattened baking cups. Position on stand. Each serves 1.

Letter Perfect Brownies

Pans: Silicone Brownie Bites Mold, Cookie Sheet, Cooling Grid

Also: Letters & Numbers Gum Paste & Fondant Mold Set, Dark Cocoa Candy Melts, Parchment Triangles, White Nonpareils Sprinkle Decorations, Disposable Decorating Bags, plastic ruler, knife, waxed paper

In advance: Make candy monograms. Using melted candy in cut disposable bag, pipe in first level of letter mold. Refrigerate until firm; unmold.

Bake and cool brownies in silicone mold supported by cookie sheet; unmold. Cover with melted candy (p. 12); let set. With melted candy in cut bag, pipe a line around bottom edge of brownie; immediately attach nonpareils. Attach monogram to top with dots of melted candy. Each serves 1.

Initially Yours

Pans: 9 x 9 x 2 in. Covered Brownie, Cooling Grid

Also: Blue Candy Melts, Brownie Fudge Icing, Vanilla Crème Drizzle Icing, Letters & Numbers Gum Paste & Fondant Mold Set, Perfect Cut Brownie Cutter, Disposable Decorating Bags, plastic ruler, paring knife, spatula

In advance: Make candy monogram. Using melted candy in cut disposable bag, pipe in first level of letter mold; refrigerate until firm and unmold.

Bake a 9 in. square brownie, about 1 in. high in pan; cool. Score 2½ in. squares with brownie cutter, cut with knife. Ice top smooth with Fudge Icing. Decorate with Drizzle Icing zigzags; position letter.

Grand Monogram

Pan: 9 x 9 x 2 in. Covered Brownie

Also: Brownie Fudge Icing, Disposable Decorating Bags, Letters & Numbers Gum Paste & Fondant Mold Set, Circle Metal Cutter, Pink Candy Melts, Pink Dusting Sugar, Sugar Shaker, Flower Nail No. 7, scissors

In advance: Make candy monogram. Using melted candy in cut disposable bag, pipe in first level of letter mold. Refrigerate until firm; unmold.

Bake and cool 9 in. square brownie; remove from pan. Cut brownies using circle cutter. Ice smooth with Fudge Icing; let icing crust. Just before serving, position flower nail, flat side down, in center of brownie. Dust brownie with pink sugar. Remove nail and position monogram. Each serves 1.

Sweet Stack

Pan: 9 x 9 x 2 in. Covered Brownie
Recipes: Fudgy or Cake Brownies, p. 78; Blonde Brownies, p. 79
Also: ¼ in. wide satin ribbon (1 yard), plastic ruler

Bake and cool 9 in. square chocolate and 9 in. square blonde brownies; remove from pan. For each treat, cut a 1 in. and 3 in. square of chocolate brownie and a 2 in. square of blonde brownie. Stack brownies and wrap with ribbon. Each serves 1.

Fudge Filigree Cupcakes

Pans: Mini and Standard Muffin, Cooling Grid
Tip: 2
Also: Brownie Fudge Icing, Light Cocoa Candy Melts, Cake Board, Brownie Pop Sticks, waxed paper

In advance: Make candy swirls. Using melted cocoa Candy Melts, pipe tip 2 outline swirls 1 x 1¼ in. wide with 1¼ in. tails, on waxed paper-covered board. Refrigerate until firm. Turn swirls over; repeat on back and refrigerate until firm. Make extras to allow for breakage.

Bake and cool one standard and one mini cupcake brownie for each treat. Spatula ice tops with Fudge Icing; stack mini cupcake on standard cupcake. Using stick make hole in top of mini cupcake for swirls. Insert swirls in mini cupcake. Each serves 1.

Top Tiers

Pan: 9 x 9 x 2 in. Covered Brownie

Recipes: Fudgy or Cake Brownies, p. 78; Blonde Brownies, p. 79

Candy: Heart Lollipop Mold, White and Light Cocoa Candy Melts

Also: 101 Cookie Cutters Set, Sugar Shaker, Dusting Sugar or confectioners' sugar

In advance: Make heart candy. Mold 1 heart for each treat using white or cocoa Candy Melts, following mold instructions; refrigerate until firm and unmold. Attach heart to a matching Candy Melts wafer with melted candy; refrigerate until firm. Bake and cool 9 in. square brownie and/or 9 in square blonde brownie; unmold. Cut 3 sizes of rounds using circle cutters from set. Sprinkle with sugar; stack largest to smallest rounds. Sprinkle with sugar. Position heart candy. Each serves 1.

Recipes from the Wilton Kitchen

You've already seen that the simple brownie contains a world of decorating possibilities. Now let us help you explore all the great ways you can bake up a batch!

Start with a trio of outstanding made-from-scratch recipes used for most of the decorated treats in this book. They're the 3 basics you grew up loving—dense and intense Fudgy Brownies, light and spongy Cake Brownies and vanilla-laced Blonde Brownies—but with your fresh ingredients, they've never tasted better. If you've never tasted a brownie that's not out of a box, wait until you experience these.

Chocolate is only the start of the great brownie flavors available. You'll find that brownies are the perfect partner for peanut butter, raspberries, caramel, coffee—and even chili powder! You'll also see how to serve brownies in fun new ways, from a candy-topped pizza to tempting sundaes. And because these projects have you cutting brownies into so many fun shapes, you may want to try Brownie Parfaits, Trifles and other great ways to use all those delicious leftovers (besides eating them yourself).

Fudgy Brownies

1½ cups all-purpose flour

½ teaspoon baking soda

½ teaspoon salt

⅔ cup (10⅓ tablespoons) unsalted butter or margarine

1½ cups granulated sugar

¼ cup water

4 cups (24 oz.) semi-sweet chocolate chips, divided

2 teaspoons Wilton Clear Vanilla Extract

4 eggs

Preheat oven to 350°F. Spray 13 x 9 in. pan with vegetable pan spray or Bake Easy! Non-Stick Spray.

In small bowl, combine flour, baking soda and salt. In small saucepan, melt butter and sugar with water; stir until sugar is dissolved. Add 2 cups chocolate chips; stir until melted. Remove from heat. Stir in vanilla.

In large bowl, beat eggs with electric mixer. Add chocolate mixture; mix well. Add flour mixture; stir until just combined. Stir in remaining 2 cups chocolate chips. Spread batter in prepared pan.

Bake 25-30 minutes or until toothpick inserted in center comes out almost clean. Cool completely before cutting.

Makes about 24 brownies.

Cake Brownies

1½ cups cake flour

¾ teaspoon baking powder

¼ teaspoon salt

4 ounces unsweetened chocolate, coarsely chopped

¾ cup (1½ sticks) unsalted butter or margarine, softened

1½ cups granulated sugar

3 eggs

2 teaspoons Wilton Clear Vanilla Extract

Preheat oven to 350°F. Spray 8 x 2 in. or 9 x 2 in. square pan with vegetable pan spray or Bake Easy! Non-Stick Spray.

In small bowl, combine flour, baking powder and salt. In small microwave safe bowl, melt chocolate; let cool slightly. In large bowl, beat butter and sugar with electric mixer until light and fluffy. Add eggs, vanilla and melted chocolate; mix well. Stir in flour mixture by hand; mix until just combined. Spread batter into prepared pan.

Bake 30-35 minutes or until toothpick inserted in center comes out almost clean. Cool completely on rack before cutting.

Brownies shown were decorated with Wilton Brownie Fudge Icing using tip 2D, garnished with fresh berries, mint or chocolate curls.

Makes about 16 brownies.

Blonde Brownies

1 cup all-purpose flour
1 teaspoon baking powder
¼ teaspoon salt
½ cup (1 stick) unsalted butter
1 cup firmly packed light brown sugar
2 eggs
2 teaspoons Wilton Pure Vanilla Extract
1 cup toasted pecans, coarsely chopped

Preheat oven to 350°F. Spray 8 x 2 in. or 9 x 2 in. square pan with vegetable pan spray or Bake Easy! Non-Stick Spray.

In small bowl, combine flour, baking powder and salt. In small saucepan, melt butter and brown sugar; stir until sugar is dissolved. Remove from heat and let cool about 5 minutes. Stir in eggs and vanilla; mix well.

Add flour mixture; mix until blended. Fold in pecans. Spread batter into prepared pan.

Bake 30-35 minutes or until toothpick inserted in center comes out clean. Cool completely before cutting.

Makes about 16 brownies.

Peanut Butter Brownies

1 cup all-purpose flour
1 teaspoon baking powder
¼ teaspoon salt
½ cup creamy peanut butter
6 tablespoons unsalted butter, softened
⅔ cup granulated sugar
½ cup firmly packed brown sugar
2 eggs
1 teaspoon Wilton Clear Vanilla Extract

Preheat oven to 350°F. Spray 8 x 2 in or 9 x 2 in. square pan with vegetable pan spray or Bake Easy! Non-Stick Spray.

In small bowl, combine flour, baking powder and salt. In large bowl, beat peanut butter, butter and sugars with electric mixer until light and fluffy. Add eggs, one at a time, and vanilla; mix well. Add flour mixture; mix until just combined. Spread batter into prepared pan.

Bake 30-35 minutes or until toothpick inserted in center comes out clean. Cool completely before cutting with Brownie and Treat Cutter. If desired top with Peanut Butter Drizzle Icing.

Makes about 16 brownies.

Rocky Road Brownies

¾ cup all-purpose flour

¼ teaspoon baking soda

¼ teaspoon salt

¼ cup (½ stick) unsalted butter or margarine

1½ cups (9 oz.) semi-sweet chocolate chips, divided

¾ cup granulated sugar

2 eggs

1½ teaspoons Wilton Clear Vanilla Extract

½ cup coarsely chopped peanuts, divided

2 cups mini marshmallows

⅓ cup semi-sweet chocolate chips, melted

Preheat oven to 350°F. Spray 8 x 2 in or 9 x 2 in. square pan with vegetable pan spray or Bake Easy! Non-Stick Spray.

In small bowl, combine flour, baking soda and salt. In large microwave safe bowl, melt butter with 1 cup chocolate chips. Stir in sugar, eggs and vanilla. Add flour mixture; stir until just combined. Stir in remaining ½ cup chocolate chips and ¼ cup peanuts. Spread batter into prepared pan.

Bake 20-25 minutes or until toothpick inserted in center comes out almost clean.

Sprinkle with marshmallows. Broil until marshmallows are golden brown, 1-2 minutes. Sprinkle with remaining ¼ cup peanuts; drizzle with melted chocolate.

Makes about 16 brownies.

Brownie Cheesecake

Crust:
- 1 package (about 16 oz.) brownie mix (8 in. square size)
- Eggs, water and oil to prepare mix

Filling:
- 3 packages (8 oz. ea.) cream cheese, softened
- 1 cup granulated sugar
- ¾ cup sour cream
- 6 eggs
- 1 teaspoon Wilton Clear Vanilla extract
- ¼ teaspoon Wilton No-Color Almond Extract

Preheat oven to 350°F. Spray 9 in. springform pan with vegetable pan spray or Bake Easy! Non-Stick Spray.

In large bowl, prepare brownie mix following package instructions. Spread into bottom of prepared pan. Bake 30-35 minutes or until toothpick inserted in center comes out clean. Cool completely. Turn oven down to 325°F.

In large bowl, beat cream cheese and sugar with electric mixer at medium speed until smooth and creamy, about 5 minutes. Beat in sour cream and eggs. Add vanilla and almond extracts. Pour over cooled crust. Place cheesecake in middle of oven. Fill a large pan

with hot water and place on rack underneath cheesecake.

Bake 1 hour 25 minutes or until cheesecake top is firm but mixture is still jiggly when gently shaken. Turn off oven; leave cheesecake in closed oven 30 minutes to cool down slowly. Remove cheesecake from oven and cool 1 hour. Refrigerate covered at least 4 hours or overnight.

If desired, decorate using Chocolate Buttercream Icing (p. 103). pipe tip 5 spirals and tip 21 rosette top border.

Makes about 12 servings.

Raspberry Swirl Cheesecake

Prepare crust and filling as for Brownie Cheesecake. Before baking, melt ½ cup raspberry jam or preserves; gently swirl into cheesecake batter. Bake as for Brownie Cheesecake.

Brownie Bits Cheesecake

Crust:

> **2 packages (about 16 oz.) brownie mix (8 in. square size)**
> **Eggs, water and oil to prepare mixes**

Filling:

> **3 packages (8 oz. ea.) cream cheese, softened**
> **1 cup granulated sugar**
> **¾ cup sour cream**
> **6 eggs**
> **1 teaspoon Wilton Clear Vanilla extract**
> **¼ teaspoon Wilton No-Color Almond Extract**

Preheat oven to 350°F. Spray 9 in. springform pan and 8 x 2 in. or 9 x 2 in. square pan with vegetable pan spray or Bake Easy! Non-Stick Spray.

In large bowl, prepare one brownie mix following package instructions. Spread into bottom of prepared square pan. In second large bowl, prepare remaining brownie mix following package instructions. Spread into prepared springform pan. Bake both pans together for 35-40 minutes or until toothpick inserted in center comes out clean. Cool completely. Turn oven down to 325°F.

Cut approximately half of the brownies from the square pan into ¾ in. pieces (about 1½ cups); set aside.

In large bowl, beat cream cheese and sugar with electric mixer at medium speed until smooth and creamy, about 5 minutes. Beat in sour cream and eggs. Add vanilla and almond extracts. Gently stir in ½ cup of the cut brownies. Pour over cooled crust. Sprinkle remaining cut brownies over cheesecake batter; lightly press into batter. Place cheesecake in middle of oven. Fill a large pan with hot water and place on rack underneath cheesecake.

Bake 1 hour 25 minutes or until cheesecake is firm on top but filling is still jiggly when gently shaken. Turn off oven; leave cheesecake in closed oven 30 minutes to cool down slowly. Remove cheesecake from oven and cool 1 hour. Refrigerate covered at least 4 hours or overnight.

Makes about 12 servings.

**Butter Pecan
Brownie Shortcake**

**Peach Melba
Brownie Shortcake**

**Banana Split
Brownie Shortcake**

**Turtle Sundae
Brownie Shortcake**

Brownie Shortcakes

1 package (about 20 oz.) brownie mix (13 x 9 in. size)
Eggs, water and oil to prepare mix

Preheat oven to 325°F. Spray Dessert Shell pan with vegetable pan spray or Bake Easy! Non-Stick Spray.

In large bowl, prepare brownie mix following package instructions. spoon into cavities of prepared pan.

Bake 35-38 minutes; set aside to cool. Fill as desired, using variations below.

Turtle Sundae Brownie Shortcake:

3 cups vanilla ice cream
¾ cup caramel ice cream topping
6 tablespoons chopped pecans or Wilton Turtle Crunch
¾ cup thawed frozen whipped topping

Top each shell with ½ cup vanilla ice cream. Drizzle with 2 tablespoons caramel sauce, 1 tablespoon pecans or Turtle Crunch and 2 tablespoons whipped topping.

Banana Split Brownie Shortcake:

3 cups strawberry ice cream
¾ cup chocolate or fudge ice cream topping
2 bananas, sliced
¾ cup thawed frozen whipped topping
6 maraschino cherries, optional

Top each shell with ½ cup strawberry ice cream. Drizzle with 2 tablespoons chocolate topping, banana slices and 2 tablespoons whipped topping. Top, if desired, with a cherry.

Peach Melba Brownie Shortcake:

3 cups peach ice cream
¾ cup raspberry syrup or ice cream topping
¾ cup thawed frozen whipped topping

Top each shell with ½ cup peach ice cream. Drizzle with 2 tablespoons raspberry syrup and 2 tablespoons whipped topping. Top, if desired, with a fresh raspberry and mint.

Butter Pecan Brownie Shortcake:

3 cups butter pecan ice cream
¾ cup butterscotch ice cream topping
¾ cup thawed frozen whipped topping

Top each shell with ½ cup butter pecan ice cream. Drizzle with 2 tablespoons butterscotch topping and 2 tablespoons whipped topping. Top, if desired, with a pecan.

Makes 6 servings.

Brownie Parfaits

1 package (about 4 oz.) vanilla instant pudding
2 cups cold milk
3 cups crumbled brownies, divided
½ cup thawed frozen whipped topping, divided

In medium bowl, prepare pudding according to package directions with milk. Refrigerate 5-10 minutes or until slightly thickened.

In each of four dessert dishes, layer crumbled brownies, ½ cup pudding and additional crumbled brownies. Top with 2 tablespoons whipped topping. Refrigerate at least 1 hour before serving.

Makes 4 servings.

Variation: Substitute your favorite instant pudding flavor (chocolate, white chocolate, cheesecake, pistachio) for the vanilla instant pudding.

Marble Cheesecake Brownies

Cheesecake Batter:
- 1 package (8 oz.) cream cheese, softened
- ¼ cup granulated sugar
- 1 egg
- ¼ teaspoon Wilton No-Color Almond Extract
- 1 cup milk chocolate chips

Brownie Batter:
- ⅔ cup all-purpose flour
- ½ teaspoon baking powder
- ¼ teaspoon salt
- ¼ cup (½ stick) unsalted butter
- 1 cup semi-sweet chocolate chips
- ½ cup granulated sugar
- 2 eggs
- ½ teaspoon Wilton Clear Vanilla Extract

Preheat oven to 350°F. Spray 8 x 2 in. or 9 x 2 in. square pan with vegetable pan spray or Bake Easy! Non-Stick Spray.

In large bowl, beat cream cheese and sugar with electric mixer until light and creamy. Add egg and almond extract; mix well. Stir in milk chocolate chips; set aside.

In small bowl, combine flour, baking powder and salt; set aside. In medium microwave safe bowl, melt butter and semi-sweet chocolate chips. Stir in sugar, eggs and vanilla; mix well. Add flour mixture; mix until just combined. Alternate dropping spoonfuls of brownie and cheesecake batter in prepared pan. Swirl the two batters together to create a marbled effect using a knife.

Bake 30-35 minutes or until toothpick inserted in center comes out clean. Cool completely before cutting.

Makes about 16 brownies.

Mocha Brownies with Mocha Ganache

Brownie:
- 1½ cups all-purpose flour
- ½ teaspoon salt
- 1 cup (2 sticks) unsalted butter
- 5 ounces unsweetened chocolate, coarsely chopped
- 2 cups granulated sugar
- 1 tablespoon instant coffee granules
- 4 eggs
- 1½ teaspoons Wilton Clear Vanilla Extract
- ¾ cup semi-sweet chocolate chips

Ganache:
- 1 teaspoon instant coffee granules
- 2 teaspoons water
- 1½ cups semi-sweet chocolate chips
- 1 cup heavy whipping cream, heated to boiling

Preheat oven to 350°F. Spray 13 x 9 in. pan with vegetable pan spray or Bake Easy! Non-Stick Spray.

In small bowl, combine flour and salt. In large microwave safe bowl, melt the butter and chopped chocolate. Stir in sugar and coffee. Add eggs and vanilla; mix well. Stir in flour mixture; mix until just combined. Stir in chocolate chips. Spread batter into prepared pan.

Bake 25-30 minutes or until toothpick inserted in center comes out almost clean. Cool completely.

For ganache, combine coffee granules with water in small bowl; stir until dissolved. In medium bowl, place chocolate; pour hot cream over chocolate. Let stand 1 minute; stir until chocolate is dissolved. Stir in coffee mixture. Pour ganache over cooled brownies. If desired, garnish with chocolate curls.

Makes about 24 brownies.

Turtle Brownies

- 2 cups all-purpose flour
- ½ teaspoon salt
- 1½ cups (3 sticks) butter, cut into pieces
- 4 squares (4 oz.) unsweetened chocolate, chopped
- 1½ cups granulated sugar
- 5 eggs, lightly beaten
- 2 teaspoons Wilton Clear Vanilla Extract
- ¾ cup toasted chopped pecans, divided
- ¾ cup semi-sweet chocolate chips
- ¾ cup toffee chips
- ½ cup caramel ice cream topping

Preheat oven to 350°F. Spray 13 x 9 in. pan with vegetable pan spray or Bake Easy! Non-Stick Spray.

In small bowl, combine flour and salt. In large microwave safe bowl, melt the butter and chocolate. Stir in sugar. Add eggs and vanilla extract; mix well. Stir in flour mixture; mix until just combined. Stir in ¼ cup pecans, chocolate chips and toffee chips. Spread batter evenly into prepared pan. Sprinkle remaining ½ cup pecans evenly over top.

Bake 35-40 minutes or until toothpick inserted in center comes out clean. Cool completely. If desired, cover half of brownie with Vanilla Créme Drizzle Icing; drizzle other half with caramel topping.

Makes 24 brownies.

Brownie Cookie Bites

1¼ cups all-purpose flour

½ teaspoon baking powder

½ teaspoon salt

⅓ cup (5⅓ tablespoons) unsalted butter, cut into pieces

2 ounces unsweetened chocolate, chopped

1 cup granulated sugar

2 eggs

1 teaspoon Wilton Clear Vanilla Extract

½ cup coarsely chopped pecans

Preheat oven to 350°F.

In small bowl, combine flour, baking powder and salt. In medium microwave safe bowl, melt butter and chocolate. Stir in sugar. Add eggs and vanilla; mix well. Add flour mixture; mix until blended. Stir in pecans. Drop dough by rounded teaspoons on ungreased cookie sheet.

Bake 8-10 minutes. Cool completely on wire rack.

Makes about 3 dozen cookies.

Frozen Raspberry Brownie Cake

1 package (about 20 oz.) brownie mix (13 x 9 in. size)

1 package (about 16 oz.) brownie mix (8 x 8 in. size)

Eggs, water and oil to prepare mixes

1 quart raspberry sherbet, softened

3 cups Chocolate Buttercream Icing (p. 103)

Preheat oven to 325°F. Spray Fanci-Fill Pans with vegetable pan spray or Bake Easy! Non-Stick Spray.

Prepare brownie mixes following package instructions for cake-like brownies. Combine brownie batters, mixing well before dividing evenly between prepared pans.

Bake 35-38 minutes or until toothpick inserted in center comes out with a few crumbs. Cool in pan on wire rack 10 minutes; remove from pan and cool completely.

Spoon softened sherbet into cavities of cooled cakes. Freeze until sherbet has hardened slightly,

about ½ hour. Assemble cake by inverting top layer onto bottom layer. Ice with chocolate buttercream icing. Freeze 8 hours or overnight. Remove from freezer 20 minutes before cutting and serving.

If desired, before cutting and serving, heat Brownie Fudge Icing following package directions. Pour over cake to glaze; garnish with fresh raspberries.

Makes 8-10 servings.

Brownie Trifle

1 package (about 16 oz.) brownie mix
  (8 in. square size)
  Eggs, water and oil to prepare mix
1 package (5.1 oz.) chocolate instant pudding mix
2 cups cold milk
6 cups thawed frozen whipped topping, divided
4 cups sliced fresh strawberries
½ cup chopped chocolate candy bars

Preheat oven to 350°F. Spray 8 x 2 in. or 9 x 2 in. square pan with vegetable pan spray or Bake Easy! Non-Stick Spray.

In large bowl, prepare brownie mix following package instructions. Spread into bottom of prepared pan.

Bake 20-25 minutes; set aside to cool completely. Cut into bite-size pieces.

In large bowl, prepare pudding mix according to package instructions using only 2 cups of milk. Chill 5-10 minutes or until slightly thickened. Gently fold in 2 cups whipped topping.

In 3-quart trifle or other clear bowl, place half the brownie pieces. Top with ½ of the pudding mixture, ½ of the remaining whipped topping and ½ of the sliced strawberries. Repeat layers with remaining ingredients. Sprinkle with chopped chocolate pieces.

Refrigerate at least 1 hour before serving.

Makes about 12 servings.

Variations: Substitute other fresh berries or sliced or chopped fresh fruit for the strawberries. Or substitute your favorite instant pudding mix for the chocolate instant pudding.

Peach Melba Trifle
Substitute Blonde Brownies (p. 79) for brownie mix and vanilla instant pudding mix for chocolate. Layer brownies and pudding with sliced or chopped peaches and raspberries.

Nutty Butter Trifle
Substitute Peanut Butter Brownies (p. 80) for brownie mix. Substitute banana cream instant pudding mix for the chocolate pudding. Layer as described above with sliced bananas and chopped peanut butter chocolate cups in place of the strawberries. **Note:** dip banana slices in lemon juice before layering to prevent the fruit from darkening.

Black Forest Trifle
Substitute pitted fresh, frozen or canned sweet cherries for sliced strawberries. Layer as described above.

Rocky Road Trifle
Substitute marshmallow cream for pudding; gently mix with 2 cups whipped topping and layer as described above with marshmallows, chopped chocolate pieces, slivered almonds and fudge ice cream topping.

Peanut Butter Mousse Brownie Cake

1 package (about 20 oz.) brownie mix (13 x 9 in. size)
1 package (about 16 oz.) brownie mix (8 x 8 in. size)
  Eggs, water and oil to prepare mixes
1 package (5.1 oz.) vanilla instant pudding mix
1 cup cold milk
½ cup creamy peanut butter
1 cup frozen whipped topping, thawed
2 cups Peanut Butter Buttercream Icing (p. 103)
  Chocolate shavings, optional

Preheat oven to 325°F. Spray both Fanci-Fill pans with vegetable pan spray or Bake Easy! Non-Stick Spray.

Prepare brownie mixes following package instructions for cake-like brownies. Combine brownie batters; mix well before dividing evenly between prepared pans.

Bake 35-38 minutes or until toothpick inserted in center comes out with a few crumbs. Cool in pan on wire rack 10 minutes; remove from pan and cool completely.

In medium bowl, combine pudding and milk. Whisk in peanut butter; stir until well blended. Fold in whipped topping. Fill cavities of cooled cakes with mixture. Assemble cake by inverting top layer onto bottom layer. Ice with peanut butter icing; garnish, if desired, with chocolate shavings. Chill at least 1 hour or until ready to serve.

Makes 8-10 servings.

Chipotle Brownies

1 cup all-purpose flour
¼ teaspoon salt
½ cup (1 stick) unsalted butter or margarine
2 ounces unsweetened chocolate, coarsely chopped
2 ounces semi-sweet chocolate, coarsely chopped
1 cup firmly packed brown sugar
1 teaspoon ground cinnamon
¾ teaspoon ground chipotle chili powder

3 eggs
½ teaspoon Wilton Clear Vanilla Extract
¼ teaspoon Wilton No-Color Almond Extract
½ cup semi-sweet chocolate chips

Preheat oven to 350°F. Spray 8 x 2 in. or 9 x 2 in. square pan with vegetable pan spray or Bake Easy! Non-Stick Spray.

In small bowl, combine flour and salt. In medium microwave safe bowl, melt butter and chopped chocolate. Stir in sugar, cinnamon and chipotle powder. Add eggs and extracts, mix well. Add flour mixture; mix well. Stir in chocolate chips. Spread batter into prepared pan.

Bake 25-30 minutes or until toothpick inserted in center comes out almost clean. Cool completely on rack before cutting. If desired, sprinkle with cocoa powder.

Makes about 16 brownies.

Peanut Butter Explosion Brownies

1 package (about 16 oz.) peanut butter cup brownie mix (8 x 8 in. size)
  Eggs, water and oil to prepare mix
1 cup creamy peanut butter
1 cup (2 sticks) butter, cut into small pieces
2 teaspoons Wilton Clear Vanilla Extract
3¼ cups confectioners' sugar
½ cup lightly salted cocktail peanuts, coarsely chopped
16 miniature peanut butter cups, cut into quarters (optional)

Preheat oven to 350°F. Spray 8 x 2 in. or 9 x 2 in square pan with vegetable pan spray or Bake Easy! Non-Stick Spray.

In large bowl, prepare brownie mix following package instructions. Spread into bottom of prepared pan.

Bake 25-30 minutes; set aside to cool for 30 minutes.

In large microwave safe bowl, melt peanut butter and butter on high 1½ minutes or until mixture begins to bubble; stir until smooth. Microwave an additional 1½ minutes. Stir in vanilla. Gradually add confectioners' sugar, stirring until smooth. Evenly spread mixture over cooled brownies. Sprinkle with peanuts and, if desired, peanut butter cups. Cover and chill 2-3 hours or until peanut butter mixture is firm.

Makes about 16 brownies.

The Ultimate Quadruple Chocolate Brownie

1½ cups all-purpose flour

½ teaspoon salt

1 cup (2 sticks) unsalted butter

4 ounces unsweetened chocolate, coarsely chopped

2 cups granulated sugar

4 eggs

1½ teaspoons Wilton Clear Vanilla Extract

¾ cup semi-sweet chocolate chips

¾ cup milk chocolate chips

¾ cup white chocolate chips

Preheat oven to 350°F. Spray 13 x 9 in. pan with vegetable pan spray or Bake Easy! Non-Stick Spray.

In small bowl, combine flour and salt. In large microwave safe bowl, melt butter and chopped chocolate. Stir in sugar, eggs and vanilla extract; mix well. Add flour mixture; mix until just combined. Stir in chips. Spread into prepared pan.

Bake 25-30 minutes or until toothpick inserted in center comes out almost clean. Cool completely on rack before cutting.

Makes about 24 brownies.

Brownie Ice Cream Roll

½ cup all-purpose flour

½ cup cocoa powder, divided

1 teaspoon baking powder

¼ teaspoon salt

4 eggs, separated

1 tablespoon cold water

¾ cup granulated sugar, divided

½ teaspoon Wilton Clear Vanilla Extract

½ teaspoon Wilton No-Color Almond Extract

½ gallon vanilla ice cream, softened

Preheat oven to 350°F. Line 18 x 12 x 1 in. jelly roll pan with parchment paper; set aside.

In medium bowl, combine flour, ¼ cup cocoa, baking powder and salt; mix well.

In large bowl, beat egg whites and water with electric mixer until frothy. Gradually add ½ cup sugar and beat until stiff peaks form; set aside. In a second large bowl, beat egg yolks until thick. Gradually add remaining sugar and extracts; beat well. Fold into egg whites. Gently fold in flour mixture. Spread mixture evenly into prepared pan.

Bake 15-18 minutes or until toothpick inserted in center comes out clean. Remove from oven to cooling rack; cool 5 minutes in pan. Sprinkle dish towel with remaining ¼ cup cocoa powder. Turn brownie onto towel. Immediately peel away parchment paper from warm brownie surface; starting at short end, roll up brownie and towel in jelly-roll fashion. Place roll seam-side down on cooling rack; cool 20 minutes.

Carefully unroll brownie. Spread ice cream over brownie to ½ inch from edges. Re-roll (without towel) in jelly roll fashion. Wrap roll in aluminum foil; freeze at least 8 hours or overnight. When ready to serve, trim ½ inch from ends of roll. Slice and serve immediately. If desired, sprinkle roll with confectioners' sugar before slicing. Freeze any remaining servings.

Makes about 10 servings.

Variation: If desired, cake can be iced with buttercream icing before freezing.

Caramel Macadamia Nut Brownies

Brownies:
- 1 cup all-purpose flour
- 1 teaspoon baking powder
- ¼ teaspoon salt
- ½ cup (1 stick) unsalted butter
- 1 cup firmly packed light brown sugar
- 2 eggs
- 2 teaspoons Wilton Pure Vanilla Extract
- ½ cup coarsely chopped toasted macadamia nuts, divided
- ½ cup toasted shredded coconut, divided

Caramel Topping:
- 30 caramels, unwrapped
- 1 tablespoon milk

Preheat oven to 350° F. Spray 8 x 2 in. or 9 x 2 in. square pan with vegetable pan spray or Bake Easy! Non-Stick Spray.

In small bowl, combine flour, baking powder and salt; set aside. In small saucepan, melt butter and brown sugar. Remove from heat; let cool about 5 minutes. Stir in eggs and vanilla; mix well. Add flour mixture; stir just until combined. Stir in ¼ cup macadamia nuts and ¼ cup coconut. Spread batter into prepared pan.

Bake 30-35 minutes or until toothpick inserted in center comes out clean. Place on wire rack and cool for at least 1 hour.

In small microwave safe bowl, melt caramels and milk. Spread over cooled brownies; sprinkle with remaining ¼ cup macadamia nuts and ¼ cup coconut. Cool completely before cutting.

Makes about 16 brownies.

Grasshopper Brownies

Brownies:
- ½ cup (I stick) unsalted butter, softened
- 2 ounces unsweetened chocolate, coarsely chopped
- I cup granulated sugar
- 2 eggs
- ½ teaspoon Wilton Clear Vanilla Extract
- ¾ cup all-purpose flour

Mint Filling:
- 3 tablespoons butter, softened
- 1½ cups confectioners' sugar
- 2 tablespoons milk
- 2-3 drops Wilton Crème de Menthe Candy Flavoring or ¼ teaspoon mint extract
- Wilton Leaf Green or Kelly Green Icing Color

Topping:
- 3 tablespoons butter
- ½ cup semi-sweet chocolate chips
- Crème de Menthe thin candies, finely chopped

Preheat oven to 350°F. Spray 8 x 2 in. or 9 x 2 in. square pan with vegetable pan spray or Bake Easy! Non-Stick Spray.

In medium microwave safe bowl, melt butter and chopped chocolate. Stir in sugar. Add eggs and vanilla; mix well. Add flour; mix until just combined. Spread batter into prepared pan.

Bake 15-20 minutes or until toothpick inserted in center comes out almost clean. Cool completely in pan.

For filling, beat butter, confectioners' sugar and milk with electric mixer in small bowl until light and fluffy. Stir in candy flavoring and icing color. Spread evenly over the cooled brownies; chill until set.

For topping, melt butter and chocolate chips in small microwave safe bowl, stirring until smooth. Cool slightly; spoon over the mint layer. Sprinkle with chopped candies. Cover and chill at least I hour before cutting.

Makes about 16 brownies.

Variation: For a quick version, top with Wilton Mint Drizzle Icing and Brownie Fudge Icing heated to make a pourable glaze.

Brownie Cobbler

2 cans (21 oz. ea.) cherry pie filling

1 cup all-purpose flour

½ cup plus 1 tablespoon granulated sugar, divided

2 tablespoons cocoa powder

1½ teaspoons baking powder

¼ cup (½ stick) unsalted butter, cut into small pieces

½ cup milk

½ teaspoon Wilton Clear Vanilla Extract

¼ cup chopped nuts (optional)

Vanilla ice cream or whipped cream

Preheat oven to 350°F. Spray 13 x 9 in. pan with vegetable pan spray or Bake Easy! Non-Stick Spray. Spread cherry pie filling in bottom of pan. Set aside.

In large bowl, combine flour, ½ cup sugar, cocoa powder and baking powder. Blend in butter using pastry blender until mixture resembles coarse crumbs. Combine milk and vanilla; add all at once to flour mixture, stirring with fork just until dough comes together. Drop by rounded tablespoons randomly over cherry filling. Sprinkle with remaining tablespoon sugar and, if desired, nuts.

Bake 30-35 minutes or until cherries are bubbly and brownie mixture is baked through. Serve warm with a scoop of vanilla ice cream or whipped cream.

Makes about 18 servings.

Brownie Layer Ice Cream Cake

Brownie:
- **2 packages (about 16 oz. ea.) brownie mix (8 x 8 in.)**
- **Eggs, water and oil to prepare mixes**

Topping:
- **1 cup caramel ice cream topping**
- **2 quarts vanilla fudge swirl ice cream, slightly softened**
- **1 cup chocolate ice cream topping**
- **1 cup caramel ice cream topping**
- **½ cup chopped nuts**

Preheat oven to 350°F. Line 13 x 9 in. pan with parchment paper, extending paper 2 inches above edge of pan; spray with vegetable pan spray or Bake Easy! Non-Stick Spray.

In large bowl, prepare 1 brownie mix following package instructions; pour into prepared pan. Bake 15-20 minutes or until toothpick inserted in center comes out with just a few crumbs attached. Cool completely in pan on wire rack. Remove brownie from pan using parchment paper to lift from the pan. Set aside. Repeat with second brownie mix; do not remove brownie from pan after cooling.

Drizzle caramel ice cream topping onto cooled brownies in pan. Spread softened ice cream evenly over brownie. Cut or crumble remaining brownie into bite-size pieces. Place brownie pieces over ice cream layer. Drizzle with chocolate and caramel ice cream topping and sprinkle with chopped nuts. Cover and freeze until firm, at least 4 hours.

Makes about 20 servings.

Candy & Brownie Pizza

Black Forest
Brownie Pizza

Rocky Road
Brownie Pizza

Peanut Butter
Brownie Pizza

Brownie Pizza

1 package (about 16 oz.) brownie mix (8 x 8 in. size)
Eggs, water and oil to prepare mix

Preheat oven to 350°F. Spray 12 in. pizza pan with vegetable pan spray or Bake Easy! Non-Stick Spray.

In large bowl, prepare brownie mix following package instructions. Spread into bottom of prepared pan. Bake 15-20 minutes or until toothpick inserted in center comes out clean. Cool completely. Top as desired using suggestions below.

Makes about 12 servings.

Candy & Brownie Pizza

1 cup assorted toppings (candy-coated chocolate candies; chocolate, butterscotch, or white chocolate chips; mini marshmallows, chopped nuts; etc.)
1 cup Wilton Dark Cocoa Candy Melts, melted

Sprinkle brownie crust with toppings. Drizzle with melted Candy Melts.

Black Forest Brownie Pizza:

1 package (8 oz.) cream cheese, softened
⅓ cup granulated sugar
1 teaspoon Wilton Clear Vanilla Extract
1 can (21 oz.) cherry pie filling
⅓ cup Wilton Dark Cocoa Candy Melts, melted

In large bowl, beat cream cheese and sugar with electric mixer at medium speed until smooth and creamy. Add vanilla; mix well. Spread over brownie crust. Top with cherry pie filling; drizzle with melted Candy Melts. Chill until ready to serve.

Rocky Road Brownie Pizza

¾ cup miniature marshmallows
½ cup chopped peanuts
½ cup chocolate chips
1 cup Wilton Dark Cocoa Candy Melts, melted

Sprinkle with marshmallows, peanuts and chocolate chips. Drizzle with melted Candy Melts.

Peanut Butter Brownie Pizza

½ package (4 oz.) cream cheese, softened
½ cup creamy peanut butter
¼ cup granulated sugar
¼ teaspoon Wilton Clear Vanilla Extract
2 tablespoons milk
1 cup assorted toppings (chopped peanut butter cups, chocolate chips, peanut butter chips, chopped peanuts, etc.)
⅓ cup Wilton Dark Cocoa Candy Melts, melted

In large bowl, beat cream cheese, peanut butter and sugar with electric mixer at medium speed until smooth and creamy. Add vanilla and milk; mix well. Spread onto brownie crust. Sprinkle with toppings and drizzle with melted Candy Melts. Chill until ready to serve.

Quick Chocolate Mousse

2 tablespoons butter, softened
½ package (4 oz.) cream cheese, softened
½ cup confectioners' sugar
½ teaspoon Wilton Clear Vanilla Extract
1 package (3.9 oz.) instant chocolate pudding mix
1½ cups milk
½ container (6 oz.) frozen whipped topping, thawed

In large bowl, combine butter, cream cheese, confectioners' sugar and vanilla. Beat on low speed to mix, then beat on medium speed until smooth. Add pudding mix and milk to bowl. Beat on low speed to combine. Fold whipped topping into pudding mixture.

Makes 4-6 servings.

Used for *A Worm Welcome*, p. 59

Berry Brownies

1 cup all-purpose flour

¼ teaspoon salt

¾ cup (1½ sticks) unsalted butter or margarine

4 ounces unsweetened chocolate, coarsely chopped

1⅓ cups granulated sugar

3 eggs

⅓ cup raspberry jam

⅛ teaspoon Wilton Artificial Raspberry Candy Flavoring or 1 teaspoon raspberry extract

½ teaspoon Wilton Clear Vanilla Extract

½ cup semi-sweet chocolate chips

½ cup milk chocolate chips

Preheat oven to 350°F. Spray 8 x 2 in or 9 x 2 in. square pan with vegetable pan spray or Bake Easy! Non-Stick Spray.

In small bowl, combine flour and salt. In large microwave safe bowl, melt butter and chopped chocolate. Stir in sugar, eggs, raspberry jam, raspberry flavoring and vanilla; mix well. Add flour mixture; mix well. Stir in chocolate chips. Spread batter into prepared pan.

Bake 35-38 minutes or until toothpick inserted in center comes out almost clean. Cool completely on rack before cutting. If desired, sprinkle with confectioners' sugar or Wilton Dusting Sugar and garnish with fresh raspberries.

Makes about 16 brownies.

Brownie Cupcakes

1¾ cups all-purpose flour

½ teaspoon salt

4 ounces unsweetened chocolate, chopped

1½ cups (3 sticks) unsalted butter, cut into pieces

1½ cups granulated sugar

4 eggs

2 teaspoons Wilton Clear Vanilla Extract

2 cups chopped pecans (optional)

Preheat oven to 350°F. Line standard muffin pan with baking cups or bake in Wilton Silicone Baking Cups supported by a cookie sheet.

In medium bowl, combine flour and salt. In large microwave safe bowl, melt butter and chocolate. Whisk in sugar, eggs and vanilla. Add flour mixture; mix until blended. If desired, stir in nuts. Spoon mixture evenly into baking cups.

Bake 18-20 minutes or until toothpick inserted in cupcake comes out clean. Cool cupcakes in pan on cooling rack 5-8 minutes. Remove cupcakes from pan; cool completely. Ice with Wilton Brownie Fudge Icing.

Makes about 20 cupcakes.

How to Perk Up Your Cake Mix

Most designs in this book can be created with cake as well as brownies. Even if you're using a cake mix rather than our recipes, your treats can hold a fun flavor surprise! Here are some easy ways to "doctor" up the batter:

♦ Substitute frozen juice concentrate for all or part of the water used;

♦ Add ½ to 1 teaspoon almond, coconut, lemon or other favorite extract or flavoring;

♦ Add a few drops of concentrated candy flavor.

Once you've made the batter, stir in:

♦ ¼ cup sprinkles or jimmies;

♦ ½ cup chocolate, butterscotch or peanut butter chips;

♦ ½ cup chopped nuts or shredded coconut;

♦ ½ cup chopped chocolate candy bars;

♦ 2 teaspoons freshly grated orange, lemon or lime zest;

♦ ½ cup mini gum drops (or chop big ones!);

♦ ¼ cup crushed hard candy;

♦ Raisins or chopped dried fruit

Most cake mixes make between 5 and 5¼ cups of batter, so you can also try these "add-ins" with your favorite "from scratch" recipe.

Buttercream Icing

½ cup solid vegetable shortening
½ cup (1 stick) butter, softened
1 teaspoon Wilton Clear Vanilla Extract
4 cups sifted confectioners' sugar (approx. 1 lb.)
2 tablespoons milk

In large bowl, cream shortening and butter with electric mixer until light and fluffy. Add vanilla. Gradually add sugar, one cup at a time, beating well on medium speed. Scrape sides and bottom of bowl often. When all sugar has been mixed in, icing will appear dry. Add milk and beat at medium speed until light and fluffy.

Keep icing covered with a damp cloth until ready to use. For best results, keep icing bowl in refrigerator when not in use. Refrigerated in an airtight container, this icing can be stored 2 weeks. Re-whip before using.

Makes about 3 cups icing.

Chocolate Buttercream Icing

½ cup solid vegetable shortening
½ cup (1 stick) butter, softened
½ cup cocoa powder
½ cup milk
1½ teaspoons Wilton Clear Vanilla Extract
5 cups confectioners' sugar (approx. 1¼ lbs.)

In large bowl, cream shortening and butter with electric mixer until light and fluffy. Add cocoa powder, milk and vanilla; beat well. Gradually add sugar, one cup at a time, beating well on medium speed. Scrape sides and bottom of bowl often. Continue beating at high speed until light and fluffy, about 7 minutes.

Makes about 3½ cups icing.

NOTE: For deeper chocolate color, add 1 ounce unsweetened chocolate, melted, or add brown icing color.

Peanut Butter Buttercream Icing

6 tablespoons creamy peanut butter
3 tablespoons solid vegetable shortening
3 tablespoons butter, softened
6 tablespoons milk
1 teaspoon Wilton Clear Vanilla Extract
4½ cups sifted confectioners' sugar (approx. 1 lb.)

In large bowl, beat peanut butter, shortening and butter with electric mixer until light and fluffy. Add milk and vanilla; mix well. Gradually add sugar, one cup at a time, beating well on medium speed. Scrape sides and bottom of bowl often.

For best results, keep icing bowl in refrigerator when not in use. Refrigerated in an airtight container, this icing can be stored 2 weeks. Re-whip before using.

Makes about 2¼ cups icing.

Royal Icing

3 tablespoons Wilton Meringue Powder
4 cups sifted confectioners' sugar (approx. 1 lb.)
6 tablespoons warm water

Beat all ingredients until icing forms peaks (7-10 minutes at low speed with a heavy-duty mixer, 10-12 minutes at high speed with a hand-held mixer).

NOTE: Keep all utensils completely grease-free for proper icing consistency.

When using large countertop mixer or for stiffer icing, use 1 tablespoon less water.

Thinned Royal Icing: To thin for pouring, add 1 teaspoon water per cup of royal icing. Use grease-free spoon or spatula to stir slowly. Add ½ teaspoon water at a time until you reach proper consistency.

Makes about 3 cups icing.

Basic Ganache

½ cup heavy whipping cream
1 package (14 oz.) Dark or Light Cocoa Candy Melts, chopped

Heat whipping cream in saucepan just to boiling point. Do not boil. Remove from heat and add chopped candy; stir until smooth and glossy. For a thinner ganache glaze, add 1 to 2 tablespoons additional whipping cream.

Makes about 3½ cups icing.

Brownie Products

We're raising the bar for brownies, with a complete line of products that will help you create the best-looking, most delicious brownies ever! With Wilton innovations for baking, cutting and decorating, you never have to serve a plain brownie again. In this section, you'll find just about everything you need to create the amazing brownie designs in this book. For a complete selection of decorating tips, tools, toppers and more, see your Wilton retailer, visit our website at www.wilton.com or check the latest edition of the Wilton Yearbook of Cake Decorating. Check back often—our website is updated regularly with exciting new products and current availability.

Brownie Tools

Tools designed with brownie baking in mind, with features that make mixing, cutting and serving easier.

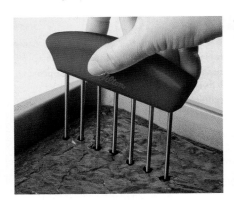

Perfect Cut Brownie Cutter

Stainless steel tines cut brownies easily with no messy edges. After removing brownie from the oven, use cutter to pre-cut your brownies. When completely cool, cut with a knife for a perfect, clean edge. 4.9 x 3.75 in.
570-1159

Sugar Shaker

Easy-to-fill, easy-to-handle shaker is great for dusting brownies and cakes with Dusting Sugar or cocoa. Fine mesh strainer with color grip and fitted lid for easy use and storage. 10 oz. capacity.
2103-388

Batter Blender

Mix thick brownie batter faster and with less effort. Silicone head is great for stirring, scraping and spreading batter. Scalloped tip breaks up clumps. Silicone heat resistant to 500°F. 11 in. long.
570-1158

Brownie & Treat Cutter

Zigzag blade cuts fun decorative edges. Works great for sandwiches, pizza, cereal treats and more. 4.9 x 3.75 in.
2308-1480

Brownie Lifter

Tapered nylon blade won't scratch non-stick pans. Shaped to fit perfectly under a cut brownie, with a deep angled handle to easily lift brownies out of the pan. 9 in. long.
570-1160

Non-Stick Bakeware

Our premium non-stick bakeware combines superior non-stick performance, serving convenience and elegant design, to provide the highest level of baking satisfaction.

6-Cavity Dessert Shell Pan
Bakes edible individual dessert dishes, great for brownie bowls, sponge cakes and more. One 8 x 8 in. size brownie mix makes 6 brownies. Individual cavities are 3.5 in. diameter x 1.5 in. deep.
2105-8600

9 in. Square Covered Brownie Pan
Perfect for taking homemade brownies to the party! Ideal size for most standard brownie mixes.
2105-9199 9 x 9 x 2 in.

8 in. Square Pan
2105-956 8 x 8 x 2 in.

Oblong Covered Cake Pan
2105-962 13 x 9 x 2 in.

Jelly Roll Pans
2105-966 Small
13.25 x 9.25 x .6 in.
2105-967 Medium
15.25 x 10.25 x .75 in.
2105-968 Large
17.25 x 11.5 x 1 in.

Pizza Pan
2105-969 12.25 in.

Jumbo Air Insulated Cookie Sheet
2105-978 18 x 14 in.

Large Air Insulated Cookie Sheet
2105-977 16 x 14 in.

8 in. Round Cake Pan
2105-957 8 x 2 in.

Cooling Grids
10 x 16 in. Rectangle
2305-228
20 x 14.5 in. Rectangle
2305-229

Mini Cupcakes 8-Cavity Pan
Bakes 4 tops, 4 bottoms. Finished cakes 3.8 x 4 in.; 6 cup total capacity. Two 8 x 8 in. brownie mixes make 4 assembled cupcakes.
2105-5043

Mini Hearts 6-Cavity Pan
Each cavity 4 in. x 2 in.; 7 cup total capacity. Two 8 x 8 in. size brownie mixes make 6 brownies.
2105-5012

Fanci-Fill Set
Create brownies and cakes with incredible flavor combinations, with these convenient non-stick pans. Set includes two 8.75 x 2 in. non-stick pans, bonus recipe booklet with 12 delicious ideas and complete instructions. Non-stick steel.
2105-150 Set/2

Aluminum Bakeware

Better bakeware means better baking results—that's why bakers and decorators have counted on Wilton for generations. Wilton aluminum bakeware is built to be the most durable and even heating—our pans will hold their shape through years of use.

Round Cake Pan
8 x 2 in. deep
2105-6136
9 x 2 in.
2105-6137
10 x 2 in.
2105-6138

Jelly Roll and Cookie Pans
Wilton pans are 1 in. deep for fuller-looking desserts.
15.5 x 10.5 x 1 in. deep.
2105-1269
18 x 12 x 1 in. deep.
2105-4854

Springform Pans
6 x 3 in. 2105-4437
8 x 3 in. 2105-8464
9 x 3 in. 2105-5354
10 x 3 in. 2105-8465

Mini Ball 6-Cavity Pan
One 8 x 8 in. size brownie mix makes 6 brownies. Six cavities, each 3.5 x 3.5 x 1.5 in. deep.
2105-1760

Teddy Bear Pan
Holds one cake mix or 1½ 13 x 9 in. size brownie mixes.
13.5 x 12.25 x 2 in deep.
2105-1193

First and Ten Football Pan
Holds one cake mix or 1½ 13 x 9 in. brownie mixes.
12 x 7.75 x 3 in. deep.
2105-6504

Jumbo Muffin 6-Cavity Pan
Make super-size cupcakes and muffins. Six cavities, each 4 x 2 in. Two 8 x 8 in. size brownie mixes make 9 brownies.
2105-1820

Standard Muffin 12-Cavity Pan
Most popular size for morning muffins, after-school cupcakes and desserts. Twelve cavities, each 3 x 1 in. Two 8 x 8 in. size brownie mixes make 15 brownies.
2105-9310

Mini Muffin
Great for mini cheesecakes, brunches, large gatherings. Cavities are 2 in. x .75 in. One 8 x 8 in. size brownie mix makes 36 brownies.
12 Cavities 2105-2125
24 Cavities 2105-9313

White Baking Cups
Jumbo 415-2503 Pk/50
Standard 415-2505 Pk./75
Mini 415-2507 Pk./100

Silicone Bakeware

Flexible silicone is ideal for releasing moist-textured brownies—they pop right out. Wilton silicone bakeware creates the perfect single servings in fun new shapes!

Brownie Pops Molds

Shaped brownies on a stick are the perfect fun-to-eat treat for parties and favors! Just bake, cool, pop in a stick and decorate.

Brownie Pops
8-Cavity Silicone Mold

One 8 x 8 in. size brownie mix makes 24 brownies. Individual cavities are 1.75 x 1.75 x 1.75 in. deep.
2105-4925

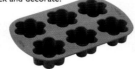

Blossom Brownie Pops
6-Cavity Silicone Mold

One 8 x 8 in. size brownie mix makes 6 brownies. Individual cavities are 2.25 x 2.25 x 1 in. deep.
2105-4924

Bite-Size Brownie Squares
24-Cavity Silicone Mold

Little brownie bites—just the right size for parties and snacks. One 8 x 8 in. size brownie mix makes 40 to 42 brownies. Individual cavities are 1.5 x 1.5 x .75 in. deep.
2105-4823

Mini Stars
6-Cavity Silicone Mold

One 8 x 8 in. size brownie mix makes 6 brownies. Pan is 10.5 x 7 in.; individual cavities are 2.5 x 2.5 x 1.25 in. deep.
2105-4819

Pastel Silicone Baking Cups

3 Pink, 3 Blue, 3 Yellow, 3 Green. Standard size, 2 in. diameter.
415-9410 Pk./12

Cutters

Combo Cutters

Make multiple shapes with just one cut. Metal Combo Cutters are divided into a neat space-saving square, which maximizes the number of treats you get from one pan. Each cutter approx. 4 x 2.5 x 2.75 in. deep. Patent pending.

Hearts
2308-1471

Mini
2308-1474

Triangles
2308-1473

Push 'N Pop!
Brownie & Treat Cutter

Cut a sensational heart-shaped treat with the stainless steel cutter and pop it out with the built-in plunger. 4.5 x 3 x 3 in. deep.
2308-4074

Comfort Grip Cutters

Easy-grip stainless steel cutters with extra-deep sides are perfect for cutting brownies and other favorite foods into spectacular shapes. Each approximately 4 x 4 x 1.75 in. Recipe included.

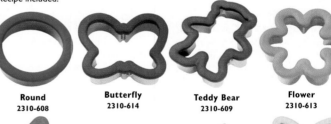

Round **2310-608** **Butterfly** **2310-614** **Teddy Bear** **2310-609** **Flower** **2310-613**

Star **2310-605** **Heart** **2310-616** **Daisy** **2310-619** **Bunny Face** **2310-626**

Witch's Hat **2310-630** **Ghost** **2310-607** **Pumpkin** **2310-600** **Egg** **2310-649**

101 Cookie Cutters

With this set, you're covered! Make cookies featuring popular holiday and theme shapes like sports, flowers, animals and more. Or use the complete alphabet and numeral collections included to create the perfect cookie message. Great for cutting all kinds of food into fun shapes—perfect for crafting, too. Average cutter size approx. 3.5 x 3.5 in. Recipe included.
2304-1050 Set/101

Mitten **2310-639** **Gingerbread Boy** **2310-602** **Santa Hat** **2310-640** **Christmas Tree** **2310-604**

Metal Cookie Cutters

Metal cutters from Wilton are built to last through years of cookie making; they cut cleanly and release with ease. Each shape is approximately 3 in.

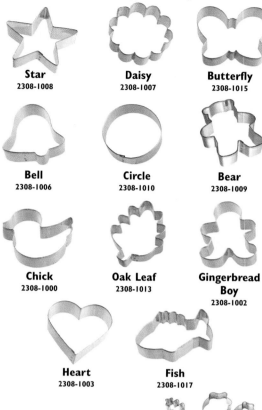

Star 2308-1008
Daisy 2308-1007
Butterfly 2308-1015
Bell 2308-1006
Circle 2308-1010
Bear 2308-1009
Chick 2308-1000
Oak Leaf 2308-1013
Gingerbread Boy 2308-1002
Heart 2308-1003
Fish 2308-1017

9 Pc. Leaves and Acorns Nesting Metal Cutter Set

Set of 9 includes graduated acorns, oak and maple leaves (3 each). 1.75 to 3.75 in. Recipe included.
2308-2000 Set/9

4 Pc. Snowflake Nesting Metal Cutter Set

Bake your favorite shapes in four fun sizes! Quality metal cuts neatly and is easy to handle. Sizes from 5 to 2.5 in.
2308-1244 Set/4

6 Pc. Valentine Mini Cutter Set

Double heart, crinkle heart, heart with arrow, heart, O and X, each approx. 1.5 in.
2308-1255 Set/6

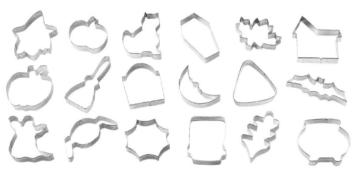

18 Pc. Holiday Cutter Set

Set of 18 includes snowflake, holly leaf, gingerbread girl, star. sleigh, tree, stocking, snowman, reindeer, ornament, candy cane, Santa hat, angel, bell, gift, wreath, gingerbread boy and mitten. Each approx. 3 in.
2308-1132 Set/18

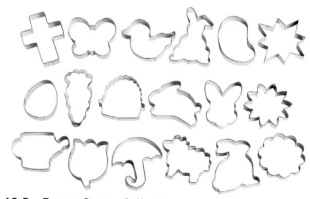

18 Pc. Halloween Cutter Set

Set of 18 includes witch, pumpkin, cat, coffin, maple leaf, house, apple, witch's broom, tombstone, moon, candy corn, bat, ghost, spider, spider web, Frankenstein, oak leaf and cauldron, each approx. 3 in.
2308-1131 Set/18

18 Pc. Easter Cutter Collection

Set of 18 includes cross, butterfly, chick, bunny, jelly bean, sun, egg, carrot, basket, leaping bunny, bunny face, daisy, sprinkling can, tulip, umbrella, lamb, rabbit and flower cutters are approx. 3 in.
2308-1134 Set/18

Cut-Outs

A great variety of shapes and sizes for cutting brownies, treats and fondant decorations. Stainless steel cutters range from .6 in. to 2.5 in..

Alphabet/Number 417-442 Set/37
Heart 417-434 Set/3
Leaf 417-437 Set/3
Flower 417-435 Set/3
Oval 417-438 Set/3
Round 417-432 Set/3
Square 417-431 Set/3

Sprinkles

Crunches

Add exciting color, taste and texture in an instant! Perfect flavor combinations for brownies; great on ice cream, too.

 Cookies 'N Cream
5 oz. bottle
710-9702

 Mint
5 oz. bottle
710-9701

Turtle
5 oz. bottle
710-9703

 Rainbow Chip
5.25 oz. bottle
710-9704

Colored Sugar

Extra-fine sugar is excellent for filling in brightly colored designs on brownies, cakes, cupcakes and cookies. 3.25 oz. bottle. Certified Kosher.

Blue
710-750

Pink
710-756

Red
710-766

Yellow
710-754

Light Green
710-752

Dark Green
710-764

 Lavender
710-758

 Orange
710-759

 Black
710-762

Cake Sparkles

Add shimmering color to brownies, cakes, cupcakes, cookies and ice cream! Brilliant edible glitter in a great variety of colors, great for stencilling, highlighting messages, snow scenes. .25 oz. Certified Kosher.

Silver
703-1285

White
703-1290

Yellow
703-1272

Purple
703-1266

Blue
703-1314

 Red
703-1284

Green
703-1278

Pink
703-1260

Orange
703-1308

Black
703-1302

Dusting Sugar

Colorful powdered sugar adds a dash of excitement to your plain brownies. Use with our Sugar Shaker (p. 104) and Brownie Stencil Set (p. 110) for a quick and easy decorating touch. 3 oz. pouch.

Blue
710-2558

Green
710-2560

Pink
710-2559

Sparkling Sugar

Put that extra dazzle in your decorating! These easy-pour sugars have a coarse texture and a brilliant sparkle that makes brownies, cupcakes, cookies and cakes really shine. 8 oz. bottle. Certified Kosher.

Lavender
710-037

Yellow
710-036

Blue
710-039

Pink
710-038

White
710-992

Jumbo Sprinkles

Give your treats a big finish! Top them with our Jumbo Sprinkles in exciting shapes and colors. These big and bold decorations are perfect for cupcakes, mini cakes, jumbo and king-size cupcakes, brownies and cookies. Certified Kosher.

Jumbo Stars
3.25 oz. bottle
710-026

Jumbo Confetti
3.25 oz. bottle
710-029

Jumbo Diamonds
3.5 oz. bottle
710-027

Jumbo Daisies
3.25 oz. bottle
710-028

Jumbo Hearts
3.25 oz. bottle
710-032

Jumbo Rainbow Nonpareils
4.8 oz. bottle
710-033

Shaped Sprinkles

Pour on the fun! Great shapes and colors add a dash of excitement to brownies, cakes, cupcakes, ice cream and more. Certified Kosher.

Rainbow Jimmies
2.5 oz. bottle
710-776

Chocolate Jimmies
2.5 oz. bottle
710-774

Rainbow Nonpareils
3 oz. bottle
710-772

White Nonpareils
3 oz. bottle
710-773

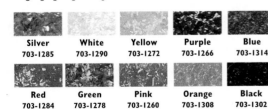 

Flowerful Medley
Includes Confetti, Colorful Leaves, Daisies, Pastel Hearts, Wild Flowers, Butterflies. 2.23 oz. bottle
710-4122

Nonpareils
Includes Pink, Orange, Green, Red, Yellow, Purple. 3 oz. total.
710-4125

Icing Colors

Wilton color is made to produce deeper, richer color by adding just a small amount. Our concentrated gel formula helps you achieve the exact shade you want without thinning your icing. You'll find a rainbow of colors, ready to blend together for creating your own custom shades.

Ivory 610-208	Daffodil Yellow‡ 610-175	Buttercup Yellow 610-216	Golden Yellow 610-159	Lemon Yellow 610-108	Copper 610-450	Creamy Peach 610-210	Rose Petal Pink 610-410	Terra Cotta 610-206	Orange 610-205	Red-Red* 610-906	Christmas Red* 610-302	Red (no-taste) 610-998	Rose 610-401

Burgundy 610-698	Pink 610-256	Violet 610-604	Delphinium Blue 610-228	Cornflower Blue 610-710	Royal Blue 610-655	Juniper Green 610-234	Brown 610-507	Sky Blue 610-700	Teal 610-207	Kelly Green 610-752	Leaf Green 610-809	Moss Green 610-851	Black* 610-981

*Note: Large amounts of these colors may affect icing taste. Use No-Taste Red for large areas of red on a cake. When using Black, start with chocolate icing to limit the amount of color needed.
‡Daffodil Yellow is an all-natural color. It does not contain Yellow #5. The color remains very pale.

Icing & Gels

Drizzle Icing

Just heat and squeeze over brownies to add a ribbon of flavor. Use with Brownie Fudge Icing for exciting marbleized designs. 10 oz. bottle. Certified Kosher.

Mint
704-152

Peanut Butter
704-150

Vanilla Crème
704-151

Brownie Fudge Icing

Rich fudge flavor and velvety texture makes this the perfect icing for spreading on brownies. Heat it in the microwave for an easy glaze; use with Wilton Drizzle Icing to create delicious designs. 1 lb. can.
710-9700

Ready-To-Use Decorator Icing

Wilton makes the only ready-to-use icing that is the perfect consistency for decorating. The pure white color is best for creating true vivid colors using Wilton Icing Colors. Rich and creamy, with a delicious homemade taste. 1 lb. can.

White 710-118
Chocolate 710-119

Pink Cookie Icing

Use this quick setting micro-wavable icing to decorate your brownies and treats with a shiny finish. Just heat and squeeze onto treats using convenient cap. Sets smooth in 45 minutes. 10 oz. bottle. Certified Kosher.
704-486

Tube Decorating Icing

The same high quality as our Ready-To-Use Decorator Icing, in a convenient tube. Colors match Wilton Icing Colors shown on p. 108. 4.25 oz. Certified Kosher.

Red 704-218	**Royal Blue** 704-248	**Pink** 704-230
Violet 704-242	**Leaf Green** 704-224	**White** 704-200
Lemon Yellow 704-236	**Kelly Green** 704-227	**Black** 704-206
Orange 704-212	**Chocolate** 704-254	

Sparkle Gel

Squeeze on sparkling color effects with our ready-to-use gel. Great for dots, messages, water effects and fondant accents. Resealable 3.5 oz. tubes. Certified Kosher.

Red 704-112
Pink 704-356
Blue 704-110
Yellow 704-108
Green 704-111

Tube Decorating Gel

Add shimmering accents, colorful highlights and sparkle to your decorating with these transparent gels. Colors match Wilton Icing Colors shown on p. 108. .75 oz. Certified Kosher.

Red 704-318	**Orange** 704-312	**White** 704-302
Pink 704-330	**Royal Blue** 704-348	**Black** 704-306
Violet 704-342	**Leaf Green** 704-324	
Lemon Yellow 704-336	**Brown** 704-354	

Candy

Candy Melts

Versatile, creamy, easy-to-melt wafers are ideal for dipping and drizzling Brownie Pops and mini treats. Their delicious taste can be varied by adding our Candy Flavors. Light and Dark Cocoa are all natural, cocoa flavor; colors are artificially vanilla flavored. 14 oz. bag. Certified Kosher.

Dark Cocoa 1911-358

Light Cocoa 1911-544

Yellow 1911-463

Orange 1911-1631

Lavender 1911-403

Blue 1911-448

Red 1911-499

Green 1911-405

White 1911-498

Pink 1911-447

Chocolate Pro Electric Melting Pot

The fast and easy way to melt chocolate and Candy Melts!

- Melting base stays cool to the touch
- Removeable non-stick Melting Pot holds 2½ cups
- Easy-pour spout
- Non-skid feet keep Chocolate Pro steady

It's the fast and fun way to mold candies like a pro. With the Chocolate Pro, you'll be able to mold lollipops and fancy dipped-center candies. Serve dipped desserts like brownie pops, fruit, cake, cookies and fondue. Add the great taste of chocolate to potato chips and pretzels. Create flavored chocolate sauces for ice cream or silky ganache glaze to pour over cakes. 120 volts. CUL Listed.
2104-9004

Candy Melting Plate

Microwave-melt up to 11 Candy Melts colors at one time with less mess! Plastic with non-slip grip edge. Includes decorating brush.
1904-8016

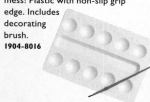

Primary Candy Color Set

Concentrated oil-based colors blend easily with Candy Melts. Includes Yellow, Orange, Red and Blue in .25 oz. jars. Certified Kosher.
1913-1299 Set/4

Garden Candy Color Set

Create pretty pastel colors! Concentrated oil-based colors blend easily with Candy Melts. Includes Pink, Green, Violet and Black in .25 oz. jars. Certified Kosher.
1913-1298 Set/4

Heart Lollipop Mold

2 designs, 8 cavities.
2115-1709

Stars Candy Mold

1 design, 12 cavities.
2115-1554

Candy Dipping Set

Easy-handling spoon and fork, each 7.75 in. long.
1904-3230 Set/2

Decorating Tools

12 Piece Brownie Decorating Set

The ideal set for discovering the fun of cake and brownie decorating! Create most of the fun icing techniques in this book with the tips included—rosettes, stars, drop flowers, messages and more. Includes tips 5, 21, 352 and 2D, standard coupler, decorating triangle, 6 disposable decorating bags and instruction sheet.
2104-2533

Deluxe Tip Set

Includes: 26 metal decorating tips (2, 4, 7, 13, 16, 17, 18, 30, 42, 46, 47, 61, 65, 66, 67, 74, 78, 97, 98, 101, 102, 103, 104, 106, 107 and 199); 1¼ in. flower nail No. 9; tip coupler; plastic tipsaver case.
2104-6666 Set/28

Featherweight Decorating Bags

Use these easy-handling bags over and over. Lightweight, strong and flexible polyester will never get stiff. Coated to prevent grease from seeping through. May be boiled; dishwasher safe. Instructions included. Sold singly.

8 in.	404-5087
10 in.	404-5109
12 in.	404-5125
14 in.	404-5140
16 in.	404-5168
18 in.	404-5184

Bake Easy! Non-Stick Spray

For treats that turn out beautifully every time, start by spraying pans with Bake Easy. This convenient non-stick spray helps your brownies and cakes release perfectly with fewer crumbs for easier icing and a flawless look for decorating.
6 oz.
702-6018

Cake Release

No need to grease and flour your baking pan—Cake Release coats in one step. Simply spread Cake Release lightly on pan bottom and sides with a pastry brush and add batter. 8 fl. oz. Certified Kosher.
702-6016

Non-Stick Parchment Paper

Use Wilton silicone-treated non-stick parchment to line baking pans and cookie sheets—a non-fat alternative that saves cleanup time. Double roll is 41 square feet, 15 in. wide. Certified Kosher.
415-680

Standard Decorating Coupler

Makes it easy to change decorating tips on the same icing bag. Fits all decorating bags and standard tips.
411-1987

Disposable Decorating Bags

Just use, then toss. Strong, flexible plastic. 12 in. size fits standard tips and couplers. Also perfect for melting Candy Melts in the microwave. Instructions included.

2104-358	Pk./12
2104-1358	Pk./24
2104-1273	Pk./50
2104-1249	Pk./100

Piping Gel

Pipe messages and designs or glaze treats before icing. Use clear or tint with icing color. 10 oz. Certified Kosher.
704-105

Meringue Powder

Primary ingredient for royal icing. Stabilizes buttercream, adds body to boiled icing and meringue. Replaces egg whites in many recipes. Certified Kosher.

4 oz. can	702-6007
8 oz. can	702-6015
16 oz. can	702-6004

No-Color Almond Extract

2 fl. oz. 604-2126

Clear Vanilla Extract

2 fl. oz. 604-2237

Brownie Stencil Set

With 6 fun designs, it's easy to make homemade brownies look great for the party or for giving. Decorate small or large pans or a single brownie. Just place stencils on iced brownies and sprinkle Dusting Sugar or Cake Sparkles over design areas.
417-1312

Brownie Sticks

For fun brownie pops.
12 in. 1912-1003 Pk./20

Flower Nail No. 7

For basic flower making. provides the control you need when piping icing flowers. Just rotate the nail between your thumb and fingers as you pipe a flower on the head. Stainless steel. 1.5 in.
402-3007

Cake Boards

Strong corrugated cardboard for strength and stability

Circles

6 in.	2104-64	Pk./10
8 in.	2104-80	Pk./12
10 in.	2104-102	Pk./12
12 in.	2104-129	Pk./8
14 in.	2104-145	Pk./6
16 in.	2104-160	Pk./6

Rectangles

10 x 14 in.	2104-554	Pk./6
13 x 19 in.	2104-552	Pk./6

Cookie Treat Sticks

For fun cookie pops.
6 in. 1912-9319 Pk./20

Decorating Triangle

Each side adds a different contoured effect to iced cakes. Easy to hold. Plastic, 5 x 5 in.
417-162

Fanci-Foil Wrap

Serving side has a non-toxic grease-resistant surface. FDA-approved for use with food. Continuous roll: 20 in. x 15 ft.

White	804-191
Gold	804-183
Silver	804-167

Letters & Numbers Gum Paste & Fondant Mold Set

With this set, it's easy to put the finishing touches on your cakes and brownies with a beautiful 3-dimensional message or monogram. Just fill molds with a 50/50 gum paste and fondant blend, press and smooth with tool included and release. Great for 2-tone letters and numbers, a perfect way to personalize brownies and cupcakes. Includes 11 mold sheets with 52 alphabet molds (upper and lower case A-Z), 3 punctuation marks and 10 numeral molds, stainless steel smoothing/releasing tool, molding instructions.
2104-3070 Set/13

Brownie Presentation

Mini Treat Baskets

Showcase brownies, cookies or other treats for the party or a great-looking gift. Dress them up with your favorite tissue squares, ribbons and gift bags for the perfect presentation.

Square
Includes 6 baskets.
3.5 x 3.5 x 1.5 in. high.
415-9474

Round
Includes 6 baskets.
3.5 in. diameter x 1.5 in. high.
415-9475

Brownie Gift Box Kits

Colorful window boxes, tissues and accents are the ideal way to present your gift of homemade brownies.

Medium
Includes 3 boxes 2 x 6.25 x 6.25 in., 3 bands 1.5 ft. long, 3 tissue sheets 4 x 4 in., 3 inserts, 1 sticker sheet.
415-9477 Set/3

Small
Includes 3 boxes 2 x 3.5 x 3.5 in., 3 tissue sheets 4 x 4 in., 6 stickers 1 in. diameter.
415-9478 Set/3

Tissue Squares

Stack brownies, cookies and other treats between colorful tissue squares for a pretty presentation. Looks great with our Mini Treat Baskets. Includes 12 brown, 12 red; 4 x 4 in.
1904-9002 Pk./24

Brownie Gift Bag Kit

Showcase your gift of homemade brownies in patterned bags that show off the tempting treats inside. Ribbons and tags included for a fun finishing touch. Includes 6 bags 18 x 5 x 4 in., 6 tags 2 x 2 in. and ribbon 1 ft. 6 in.
1912-1298 Set/6

Brownie Envelope Kit

Create a fun brownie gift with envelopes, lace-look doilies and colorful seals. Just lay envelope flat and place doily and brownie in center; fold flaps toward center and secure with seals. Includes 6 envelopes 4.5 x 4.5 in, 6 doilies 4.5 in. diameter, 6 seals 1.5 in. diameter.
1912-1297 Set/6

The Ultimate 3-In-1 Caddy

It's the most convenient way to take along brownies, cakes, cupcakes, muffins and more! The Ultimate 3-In-1 Caddy features an exclusive reversible cupcake tray which holds 12 standard or 24 mini cupcakes. Or, remove the tray to carry up to a 9 x 13 in. decorated cake on the sturdy locking base. The see-through cover has higher sides to protect icing flowers and tall decorations. You can also use the caddy at home, to keep pies, cookies and brownies fresh for days after baking. 17.9 x 14.4 x 6.8 in. high.
Patent No. D572,539
2105-9958

Cupcakes 'N More Dessert Stands

The twisting, towering design is perfect for any setting—showers, kids' birthdays, weddings, holidays and more. Easy to assemble, the coated metal stand has a durable non-chip finish. Collapsible design stores easily.

13 Count Dessert Stand
9.25 in. high x 9 in. wide. Holds 13 standard cupcakes.
307-831

23 Count Dessert Stand
12 in. high x 13 wide. Holds 23 standard cupcakes.
Patent Nos. 7,387,283; D516,385
307-826

Candles

Assorted Celebration Candles
2½ in. high. **Pk./24**
2811-215

Celebration Candles
2½ in. high. **Pk./24**
White **2811-207**
Pink **2811-213**
Red **2811-209**
Blue **2811-210**
Black **2811-224**

Round Celebration Candles
2½ in. high. **Pk./24**
Soft **2811-291**
Hot **2811-225**
Rainbow **2811-284**

Keeping In Touch With Wilton

There's always something new at Wilton! Fun decorating courses that will help your decorating skills soar. Exciting cake designs to challenge you. Great new decorating products to try. Helpful hints to make your decorating more efficient and successful. Here's how you can keep up to date with what's happening at Wilton.

Decorating Classes

Do you want to learn more about cake decorating, with the personal guidance of a Wilton instructor? Wilton has two ways to help you.

The Wilton School of Cake Decorating and Confectionery Art is the home of the world's most popular cake decorating curriculum. For more than 80 years, thousands of students from around the world have learned to decorate cakes using The Wilton Method. In 1929, Dewey McKinley Wilton taught the first small classes in his Chicago home. Today, The Wilton School teaches more people to decorate than any school in the world. As the school has grown, some techniques have been refined and there are more classes to choose from—but the main philosophies of the Wilton Method have remained.

The Wilton School occupies a state-of-the-art facility in Darien, Illinois. More than 120 courses are offered each year, including The Master Course, a 2-week class that provides individualized instruction in everything from borders and flowers to constructing a tiered wedding cake. Other courses focus on specific subjects, such as the Lambeth Method, Fondant Art and Tiered Cakes. Courses in Gum Paste and Chocolate Artistry feature personal instruction from well-known experts.

For more information or to enroll, write to:
Wilton School of Cake Decorating and Confectionery Art
2240 West 75th Street, Woodridge, IL 60517
Attn: School Coordinator

Or visit: www.school.wilton.com
Or call: 800-772-7111, ext. 2888, for a free brochure and schedule.

Wilton Method Class Programs are the convenient way to learn to decorate, close to your home. Wilton Method Classes are easy and fun for everyone. You can learn the fundamentals of cake decorating with a Wilton-trained teacher in just four 2-hour classes. When the course is over, you'll know how to decorate star and shell birthday cakes or floral anniversary cakes like a pro. Everyone has a good time—it's a great place for new decorators to discover their talent. Since 1974, hundreds of thousands have enjoyed these courses. Special Project Classes are also available in subjects like candy-making, gingerbread, fondant, cookie blossoms and more.

Find classes near you!
In U.S.A., call 800-942-8881 or visit www.wilton.com
In Canada, call 416-679-0790, ext. 200, or email classprograms@wilton.ca
In Mexico, visit www.wiltonmexico.com

Wilton Products

Visit a Wilton Dealer near you. Your local Wilton Dealer is the best place to see the great variety of cake decorating products made by Wilton. If you are new to decorating, it's a good idea to see these products in person; if you are an experienced decorator, you'll want to visit your Wilton Dealer regularly to have the supplies you need on hand. From bakeware and icing supplies to candles and publications, most Wilton retailers carry a good stock of items needed for decorating. Remember, the selection of products change with each season, so if you want to decorate cakes in time for upcoming holidays, visit often to stock up on current pans, colors and toppers.

Order on-line, by phone or by mail. You can also place orders 24 hours a day at our website, www.wilton.com. Shopping on-line is fast, easy and secure. Or, you can place an order by phone at 800-794-5866 (7WILTON) or by mail, using the Order Form in the Wilton Yearbook of Cake Decorating.

Wilton On The Web

www.wilton.com is the place to find Wilton decorating information on-line. It's filled with great decorating ideas and delicious recipes, updated regularly for the season. You'll also find helpful hints, answers to common decorating questions and easy shopping for great Wilton products.

Wilton Publications

We never run out of decorating ideas! Each year, Wilton publishes more new idea books based on Wilton Method techniques. When you're planning a specific occasion, Wilton books are a fantastic source of decorating inspiration.

The Wilton Yearbook of Cake Decorating is our annual showcase of the latest ideas in decorating. Each edition is packed with all-new cake ideas, instructions and products—it's the best place to find out what's new at Wilton. Cakes for every occasion throughout the year are included: holidays, graduations, birthdays, weddings and more. If you are looking for a new cake to test your decorating skills, you can't beat the Yearbook.

Wilton also regularly publishes special interest decorating books, including books on wedding and holiday decorating, candy-making, home entertaining and food gifting. Look for them wherever Wilton products are sold.